THE MULTIPLIER EFFECT

RULE OF LAW, LEADERSHIP,

AND

INSIGHTS OF NATURAL SCIENCES

Contents

Preface	iii
1 Leadership: Historical Perspective	1
2 Lawful Governance Spawns Growth	13
3 Be There	35
4 Dignity of Work	47
5 Be Aware	61
6 Hubris	78
7 Beatus Pursuit	97
8 Toxic leadership	113
9 Neuroscience and Leadership	131
10 Black Swan Events and Leadership	148
11 Impactful Leadership	163
12 Assessing Leadership	180
13 Leadership & Winning Strategies	199

14 Caged Bureaucracy: Learned Helplessness   233

Acknowledgements   247

Index   249

Preface

Nature is smart. Science laws help human beings understand it. If the laws of Nature seem to work in the physical systems, why not understand social systems consistent with natural sciences? Water flows from a higher gradient to a lower gradient till an equilibrium is reached. Electricity, too, flows from higher potential to lower potential. However, wealth does not seem to follow this simple rule. Inequality is dangerous. Wages earned by top CEOs and front-line workers seem to defy the golden ratio rule of Nature. Application of laws of natural sciences to social and governance systems help solving intricate issues people aspire to deal with.

Two gametes, one zygote, the story of life begins. Life thrives where food, shelter, and safety are in abundance. The complete absence of necessary conditions of life guarantees its extinction. The quest to know more about life and how to lead it never ended. Mathematically, physiologically, biologically, people put different perspectives to life. Mathematically, life is a utility function; physiologically, life is an ordered, functional, irreversible process; biologically, life is a structured functional organism of information molecules. Life has been defined by great people with their unique perspectives emerging out of their unique existential experiences. Shakespeare understood life as "sound and fury, signifying nothing"; physicists understand life through second laws of thermodynamics as an irreversible process of ordered particles. There can be more than a million other ways to understand life and assign a definition to it.

The essence of life, however, lies in Nature's phenomenon. Human beings are a part of this phenomenon. Homo sapiens have this Nature's unique gift of making and using tools as compared to other species. Given the fact that life exists, the question arises: how to live it great? Can an individual live life independently of other lives/species? Or does one need other lives to be a part of their world? If we cannot exist without the existence of others, then how to coexist and thrive together? The ecological system perspective of life gives us hope.

For coexistence, there comes the need for a common thread that weaves across; for coexistence, there comes the need for upholding Nature's laws given the fact that homo sapiens are existence in Nature like any other existence of life. Anything against Nature's laws then would bring pain and existential threat. If everyone understands and respects Nature's laws, there would be no need for any structure to perform the necessary compliance functions. A stateless society, the ultimate dream of self-ordered living, can be imagined. But there exists little evidence to support such an idea. States and governance do exist. Some people have the capacity and capability to understand Nature's phenomenon of existence and have the ability to lead folks toward an orderly coexistence. Good leadership holds the key for people to live and thrive.

Governance and leadership affect us all. Every citizen is a stakeholder in a democratic setup in space and time. Governance may be at a country level, management at a state level, or administration at a local level; it impacts all lives. Leadership positions are the keystones in the governance space structures. Any fragility in the keystone tells upon the system itself, and outcomes are commensurate. It matters whether leadership is directive, authoritative, or supportive to the people's concerns; it matters whether leaders are there for them; it matters if they (leaders) are aware of their problems. It matters if leaders know that it is about the people and not about them; it matters if leaders are authentic and do not walk with hubris.

The purpose is to hold them accountable by telling what their performance is, what authentic leadership is. What gets measured gets accomplished. Can we understand governance and leadership as an ecosystem and apply laws of Nature and physics? The answer is yes. For example, for governance evaluation, entropy is one notion. Entropy means disorder. If we can measure entropy in governance, then we can know how much useful work has been accomplished and how much governance energy has not been available for the useful work. By measuring entropy, we can understand the multiple effects of good acts. Good governance focuses on improving the system's effectiveness.

A historical perspective of the leadership process, work done by many great scholars on the subject have been reflected. One chapter is devoted to lawful governance. It focuses on the central idea of how safety and the rule of law are an integral part of leadership, how safety is critical to the economic equation, and how an economic equation is a part of the life equation - existence. The central idea of leadership is about making peoples' lives better, leadership has the responsibility and accountability, and leadership must work through a free flow of information to its stakeholders (people, citizens) and be consistent with transparency principles.

In the constitution of India, there exists a provision for the scientific temper. (Directive Principles, 51A. It shall be the duty of every citizen of India; (h) to develop the scientific temper, humanism, and the spirit of inquiry and reform). The scientific thought process helps to solve problems. In this book, the guiding principle has been that natural laws, which are tried and tested, have an application to social sciences and social ecosystems. Natural laws like entropy (disorder, reactance) and the physics of the domino effect (amplification of forces) have lots to offer for understanding, knowing, and solving problems of social ecosystems like governance. A good act performed is not a singular act—the singular act results in a multiplier effect. The outcome is multi times the intended impact, and the development for the whole ecosystem is beneficial.

The thing of everything is that leaders in a modern setup of republics have a contract with the people, who elect them through an election process to preserve and protect their lives, liberty, and property. The civil servants take an oath of loyalty to the constitution and not to a person at the helm of affairs. The rule of law is central to all decisions and actions of such elected and recruited leaders (state actors). By doing this small act, which they take an oath to abide by, leaders have this excellent task of making the people's lives worth living. On the contrary, if the rule of law fails to prevail, democratic institutions crumble under the pressure of the authoritarian dispositions of toxic leadership, economic hell visits people. There is no other way to lift people above the poverty levels than making "Rule of Law" prevail.

"Rule of Law" is a necessary condition for any nation, society, or locality to prosper. This is not what my opinion is; this is not what I pontificate. Instead, this is what the data speaks; this is what the pattern tells. Leadership is no good if it fails the crucible test of the "Rule of Law." My definition of leadership is in two words: "Be There:" Be there for the "Rule of Law"; be there for the people. Position and experience have the potential of firewalling good governance. Good leaders are clear, consistent, and honest in communicating with people and solve their problems. Understanding leadership with a natural sciences perspective brings forward the notion that we can measure it like any other natural phenomenon and account for it. Any deviations are dangerous to the ecosystem. And if the ecosystem is destroyed, it takes years to rebuild. Authentic leadership is about people, and we are a part of this universe in space and time, as Einstein said it. Singh. Maha

x

1

Leadership: Historical Perspective

The narrative of leadership is about people; it's about delivering desired results. According to John Maxwell, leadership has levels. In the first level, leaders make people work and get the assigned job done. People have no choice but to work. The positional style of leadership is level one. The second level of leaders fall in the category of people doing the assigned job efficiently because they like the leader. The third level of leadership is where leaders deliver. The fourth level of leadership helps people grow, and it could be equated to the coaching style of leadership. The fifth level is about authentic leadership: it's about people, and a leader represents who you are. As Gandhi Ji said, "Be the change you want to see in the world." Authentic leaders put people first and solve problems efficiently. They are aware of issues, and they are there for them.

As homo sapiens, we have challenges concerning law and order, environment, economic turmoil, education, health, and relationships, foreign and domestic. The question is, as species, how to best survive and thrive? The wellbeing of society is hardly measured: how to calculate happiness; how to measure empathy; how to measure environment loss; how to estimate our relationships; how to measure leadership; how to measure the right things and change the narrative? Certainly, it cannot be measured in terms of GDP only. Measurement of leadership for good governance is possible. For example, out of 100 issues, we may agree on 80 and differ on 20. There is an excellent area of collaboration to work on 80 and avoid conflict, which is inefficient. We may plan to resolve differences on the remaining 20. Measurement, it would appear, has the potential for a path forward and improvement over things we get stuck with. Good leadership and good governance show outcomes that are visible and measurable.

Leaders are the kind of persons who keep folks together, who bring about order in society. They are the kind of people who share a vision with the people. They are the captain of the ship; they sail together to the destination. They motivate, communicate, connect, build trust and good faith with the masses they lead. And they are capable of taking their folks out of crisis and vision them to opportunities they aspire for. Leadership involves empathy, humility, problem-solving, crisis handling, pathfinding, vision, and guts. Authentic leadership can be defined as "Be Aware; Be There." "Know Thyself," the celebrated Socratic formulation, is universally acclaimed, and it helps an individual attain good living in collective safe living. Leaders are the persons who are aware of the issues at hand and genuinely are concerned about solving problems.

Historically, generals had fought wars, applied strategies, and came home winners. Kings and Queens guided their countries through times of droughts and plenty; their subjects worshipped them and trusted them as divine construction. However, with time, collective wisdom took a different course. As of today, we have democracies. One point of convergence that prevails is that democracy is the best option as a governance mechanism. Despite concerns, people love democracies: government of the people, by the people, for the people. The rule of law, not the rule of a person, is the essence of democracy. Authentic leadership is the beacon to keep it alive and thrive.

Leadership is a process that accomplishes set goals, objectives as agreed/understood by a collective way of life for an orderly universe to avoid adversities. Narratives of charismatic leaders are passed on by the people resonating with the outcomes because of leaders' actions. Lately, with the progressive times, studies have been accomplished by studying empirical data and emerging patterns. According to Goleman, threshold capabilities go into the making of a leader: emotional intelligence, empathy, self-awareness, self-regulation, motivation, and social skills. According to Peter F. Drucker, an effective executive would always ask what needs to be done and what is suitable to be done. He emphasized being responsible for decisions and actions. According to him, the right things done are the essence of leadership. He also emphasized discipline for effectiveness, and, according to him, learning plays a significant role.

John P. Kotter, in his research on leadership, found out that corporations are over-managed and underled. So, he worked on the idea of what leaders do. He suggested that managers are responsible for planning, budgeting, organizing, staffing, control, and solving problems, whereas leaders are the providers of direction, vision, and motivation. So, leadership has this unique endowment of providing vision and direction.

Literature is replete with narratives about leadership. Socrates, Plato, Aristotle, Voltaire, et al. have provided thoughts and knowledge on societies that care for a reason. Socrates believed in a just society. According to Plato, a few wise people only can lead humanity to virtuous living. Voltaire emphasized that through the application of reason alone, people can control their destiny. The rationalist approach believed in the perfectionist qualities of human beings. However, toward the end of the nineteenth century, two great people appeared on the scene to shoot down the rationalist approach. Sigmund Freud and Max Weber hit against the rationality belief and progress. Freud's theory of psychoanalysis rests on the unconscious idea that remains buried under the rational mind. It argued that the unconscious is responsible for the fair part of the behavior of individuals. Max Weber, a critic of Marx and a great sociologist, put forward an idea against institutions' destructive forces of technical rationality. Bureaucracies have this force of dehumanizing persons at the cost of efficiency.

There are more than 100 definitions of leadership (Hockaday and Puryear, 2000). In the early 20th century, in-depth research took place, and there came a theory of leadership known as "Trait theory." According to this theory, a leader has traits that qualify him to be a leader or the qualities with which they are born. Through personality tests, these traits are identified, and a would-be leader is born. Attributes like "vision; integrity; confidence; courage; technical knowledge; collaborators, persistence; good judgment; and the desire to lead" are tested on a scale, and a certificate of leadership is awarded. There may be a hundred and ten more traits that could be included for the personality test to qualify as a CEO (leaders) of a big corporation or some big organization or an army commander. When recruitment takes place for the officers in the army and elsewhere, personality tests are standard. Without any doubt, the trait theory of leadership centers around the traits that people have built into their personalities.

However, Behavioral theories emphasize that leadership can be learned. It is not valid that leaders are born with unusual something that qualifies them to be leaders and others are bereft of those qualities. According to behavioral theory, leadership lies in leadership style, in the manner of leading people. The idea of leadership styles got steam. For instance, some leaders are people-centric, and some leaders are task-centric. In the 1940s, the democratic style of leadership caught fire. People were sent for training to lead. The hail-fellow-well-met style had its heyday. FDR trusted in open, democratic, and meritocratic leadership. So, it's the style of leading rather than being born with a set of traits. Thus, came the style theory: leadership style matters.

And then appeared the Contingency theory. According to this theory, leadership depends upon a situation. Circumstances require some skills, and a person, who displays the skill set to meet a situation, emerges as a leader. In other words, leaders emerge out of a situation. There are millions of problems that need resolutions then how many styles of leadership would be sufficient. It makes the leadership definition complex and dynamic. A good soccer captain emerges a hero who brings home a trophy; a good pilot emerges a celebrity who lands a plane safely on the water without losing a life; a captain of a ship emerges a hero who brings wrecking craft to shores; army general is sung well who comes back home victorious. Under these contingencies/situations, the essence of leadership lies in solving a crisis and helping everybody aboard to be back home safe. It's people-centric. Yes, leadership is about people. One fabric that runs across all leadership styles/contingencies is caring for the folks you lead, and the leader is endowed with the skillset under the circumstances to know and handle best. There are, indeed, some necessary conditions for leadership; however, not sufficient unless the leaders have passed the crucible test: they come home as winners, solve problems, and lay a path forward.

All theories and narratives about leadership offer something; however, no single idea or single description is sufficient or holistic to explain the complexity and dynamism of leadership people aspire to have. Professors and students at top universities of the world spare no effort in researching for the correct answer, and much research has been conducted. According to the study, authentic leadership shows some common threads (ingredients) that run through the concept of leadership. The striking facts about leadership that stand out are self-awareness, sense of wrong and right (Morality), threshold skills of handling a situation, empathy, connecting with people, passion with reason, sensing and visualizing power, standing up to a crisis with vision and guts, discipline, and control. It's about people and not for self or self-gains; not for self-aggrandizement; it's about humility, and hubris is malaise.

Thinking of toxic and authoritarian leaders, such dictators come to mind: Idi Amin, Uganda (Approx.1925-2003), Nicolae Ceausescu, Romania (1918-1989), Augusto Pinochet, Chile (1915-2006), Kim Il-sung, North Korea (1912-1994), Francois "Papa Doc" Duvalier, Haiti (1907-1971), Mao Zedong, China (1893-1976), Francisco Franco, Spain (1892-1975), Adolf Hitler, Germany (1889-1945), Joseph Stalin, Russia (1878-1953), Benito Mussolini, Italy (1883-1945). Dictators care for only themselves. Whatever comes in their way is removed with brutal force. Fear is the tool they use. Well, this kind of stuff doesn't even fall in the category of leadership. It's just toxic.

Learning curve up north, researchers have worked on frameworks to understand how the leadership process functions deeply. Structures and steps are developed surgically to know how some people succeed in some situations and fail to deliver in a separate set of circumstances. For instance, Churchill was understood to be a great leader of wartime; however, peacetime needed another skill set to lead the country. Another example: Step up -Step back framework by Dr. Elsbeth Johnson, MIT professor, is a framework for influential leaders to implement strategic changes in their organizations effectively. The critical elements in this framework are the clarity and alignment for a step up and then focus and consistency to have a degree back and enough time for the managerial team to bring home the intended outcomes.

According to Field Marshal Manek Shaw, leadership is all about men's management and resources management. It's about morals (a sense of right and wrong), character (integrity and courage), and discipline. It's about knowing self. Leadership is in shortage, according to him. He further adds, internally grounded habits of integrity, honesty, trustworthiness, humility, self-discipline are necessary conditions for leadership to thrive.

According to Warren G. Bennis and Robert J. Thomas, comparing leadership styles of those who grew to maturity during World War II with those now known as Generation X or Generation Y would seem to be an exercise in futility. Nevertheless, through a series of interviews with people who are recognized leaders of both large and small companies, the authors of *Geeks and Geezers: How Era, Values, and Defining Moments Shape Leaders* speak a lot about the similarities between two generations. It offers an insight into the traits or qualities of leadership that transcend generations.

The breakthrough discovery is that successful leaders among geeks and geezers possess the quality of "neoteny," specific youthful curiosity and joie *de vivre* that make them want to learn constantly and explore new possibilities both in their business and personal lives. Leaders from both generations exhibited exceptional "adaptive capacity," the ability to adjust their course when unforeseen difficulties arose. The ability to be adaptive was frequently put to the test early in these leaders' careers. Each went through the defining experience in their careers that tested their ability to overcome obstacles. This experience is the "crucible" in which values are tested, and people learn not merely to persevere but also to pursue their goals despite seemingly insurmountable challenges. Leadership would remain relevant and critical for a good life as it had been relevant in historic times. Captains sailed and would sail and navigate ships to shores safely. A skill set, indeed, is the essence of taking people safe to shores.

Authentic leadership's essence lies not in power and position but in connecting with people clearly and effectively. It lies in communicating consistently with a commitment to the defined goals. Authentic leaders do not use and abuse power and position for personal gains. The sublime leadership of Gandhi Ji and Nelson Mandela are super examples of authentic leaders.

Leaders do have the desire and fire to lead. Judgment, integrity, humility, vision, direction, temperament, self-awareness, non-arrogance are some of the key elements that run into the lifeline of leadership. Two words: 'vision and guts'; two words: 'be aware'; two words: 'be there, are the essence of genuine leadership. Great leaders do have the wisdom, move clearly, and act with courage. Leadership is contextual, complex, and dynamic. However, common ingredients make leadership outstand. Leadership focuses on people and their best interests. "Be Aware" and "Be There" are the keystones of authentic leadership.

****

2

Lawful Governance Spawns Growth

Governance is universally understood as how to run a government or an organization. Governance is the top-level leadership. It refers to structures and processes, institutions that are put in place to ensure law, equity, and inclusiveness. Governance means following the rules of the law that are transparent. Governance is about the holistic environment and culture where people participate and prosper. It's about vision, goals, and authority to manage economic, political, and socio-cultural affairs. However, governance is not management. Management is an accomplishment of set goals and involves planning, organizing, and control of resources. In other words, governance is leadership that captains the ship to the shore. According to international organizations, "governance has been defined to refer to structures and processes that are designed to ensure accountability, transparency, responsiveness, the rule of law, stability, equity and inclusiveness, empowerment, and broad-based participation. Governance also represents the norms, values, and rules of the game through which public affairs are managed in a manner that is transparent, participatory, inclusive, and responsive." Good governance, thus, is good leadership.

Leadership is about the order, the rule of law; it's some promise to make people emerge out of misery and a path forward to a good living; it's some certainty and control over crisis; it's some hope out of despair. And it's about people. Voltaire and his Enlightenment colleagues championed reason as the way to free people from arbitrary power and the "superstition" of religion. Good governance is part of the economic equation. Empirical data has enough evidence to suggest that rule of law, which is the primary function of good governance, is a necessary condition for the prosperity and safety of the people. A regression model with variables of law and order and prosperity provides a window on leadership and governance. What causes prosperity? The answer is law and order.

Conversely (may not be accurate, though), prosperity brings about law and order. However, law and order accompanied by freedom and justice only have meaning. In an authoritarian regime, an order may be there, but prosperity may be a distant dream. The essence of good governance is the rule of law, not the rule of a person; loyalty to the constitution – the rule book, not to a person – head of the state. Recent happenings (2021) in the USA have jolted the world and the very image of the country. It advocates for democracy and democratic institutions. Both got hit by the turbulence by a person none other than the head of the state. Two additional ingredients of a law-and-order abiding society are freedom and justice.

The countries that have great law and order and great democratic institutions have great prosperity. Data from International organizations on the subject of the law-and-order index and household income show (Figure 2.1) that peace and prosperity come together. It does not need a crystal ball to know the expected outcome. Law and order directly correlate with income. However, caution is required. Law and order in authoritarian regimes do not bring prosperity outcomes. For instance, in North Korea, there is no law-and-order issue; however, ordinary people are not free from misery. Law and order necessarily mean the coexistence of freedom and justice. Countries with high scores on law-and-order and a high prevalence of justice and liberty only bring about prosperity. The empirical question is: Is law and order a necessary condition for growth?

The relationship, shown in Figure 2.1, is in the form of a regression analysis. It becomes abundantly clear that as to the validity (for interested math readers, regression statistics are robust), no further explanation is required. It's a positive relationship: good law-and-order means good growth. Misery seems to be a thing of the past in countries where societies have preferred democratic institutions. Professor Acemoglu at MIT has researched the subject of why some countries prosper and why others don't. His findings show that it is not geography but the presence of democratic institutions that makes a difference. He explains the two Koreas' differing prosperity despite geographical conditions being not different. South Korea is prosperous, and the North suffers from misery.

FIGURE 2.1

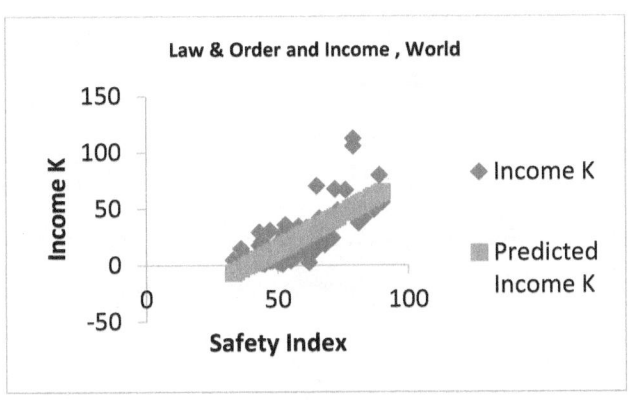

Based on data, an inescapable conclusion can be drawn that this model helps raise incomes; it helps reduce inequities; it helps collective security and thus, implicitly helps individual security. When the facts are so clear, why people still follow the path of destruction is confounding. Perhaps the answer lies in authoritarianism. Autocrats aren't answerable to anyone. The lawful, constitutional governance model is warped, twisted, diluted, distorted, disrupted by irrational, idiotic, ignorant dispositions (IIID) of narcissistic leadership. Self-gains, influence peddling, nepotism is not uncommon. Maybe an explanation lies in (REED) the Raw Expressions of Evolutionary Dispositions. For myopic self-gains and interests, some leaders bring embarrassment to themselves and the institutions they govern. Few of the indicators of law-and-order deficit states observable lie in nepotism, corruption, self- gains. In this scenario, most state actors belong to a clan, and tribalism is the apparent outcome. This gives rise to populist policies, and progressive agenda remains a mirage for the main street people. Law and order with freedom and justice should be the top priority for leaders who mean business. Any diversion from this course is dangerous.

Law and Order and Income in the States of India

In figure 2.2, we again see that the hypothesis, "good law and order means good income," is validated. In figure 2.1, the relationship between the variables of Law & Order and Income (per capita income) depicted that lawful governance generates economic growth. The same pattern is seen in the data from the states of India: the rule of law and income generation are positively correlated. States with superior law and order conditions are far more prosperous than the states with inferior law and order. Even in the same country, different regions – states, have differing law and order conditions, and so is the outcome, which is consistent with the hypothesis. In India, law and order are state subjects, which is why different states have different states of law and order. Good leadership means the excellent rule of law; the superb rule of law means good income and wellbeing.

FIGURE 2.2

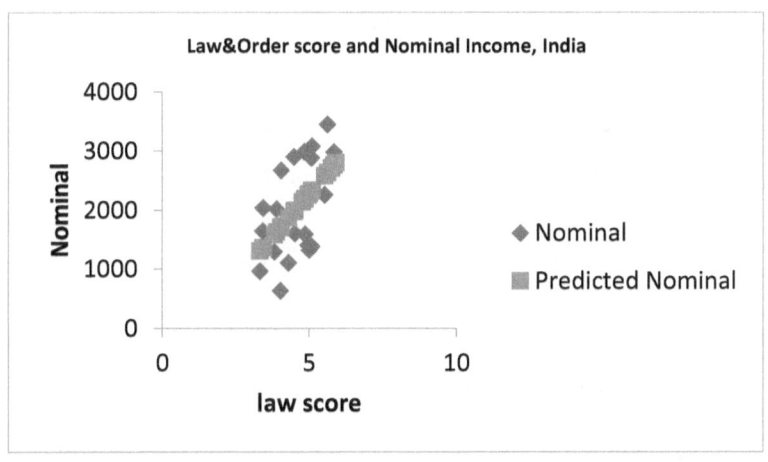

If leadership is capable of providing to its people good law and order, prosperity will follow. The states of Bihar and UP score exceptionally low on law and order and so are on the per capita income. Geographical conditions both in Bihar and UP are consistent with good natural resources. Then why people are poor in these states? Recently, in 2016-2021, though, law and order improved (crime rate fell 50-60% and income increased from ~45000 to ~94000) in the state of UP. The reason is not far to seek. Pattern hidden in the data tells tales. It's poor law and order state of affairs. Leadership in these two states seems to have not cared much for the safety and security of the people. Outcomes aren't excellent: income is low. It's a somewhat vicious circle. If we trust science and data, one thing is obvious: failed law and order is a sure recipe for poverty.

Rule of Law and House-Hold Income in the United States of America

Yet another example. Data relationship between two variables of household income and crime rate (a proxy for the rule of law) in the 50 states of the USA validate the same pattern as in general case (Figure 2.1) of all the countries and the case of the states in India (Figure 2.2). The rule of law is the key to prosperity. Without this key, we cannot open the gates of good living for the people. This is highly significant that institutions responsible for maintaining the rule of law must be in place with excellent skills. Any dilution in this idea is a sure invitation to trouble. In Figure 2.3, data tell the same story: states have lower household income and higher crime rates.

FIGURE 2.3

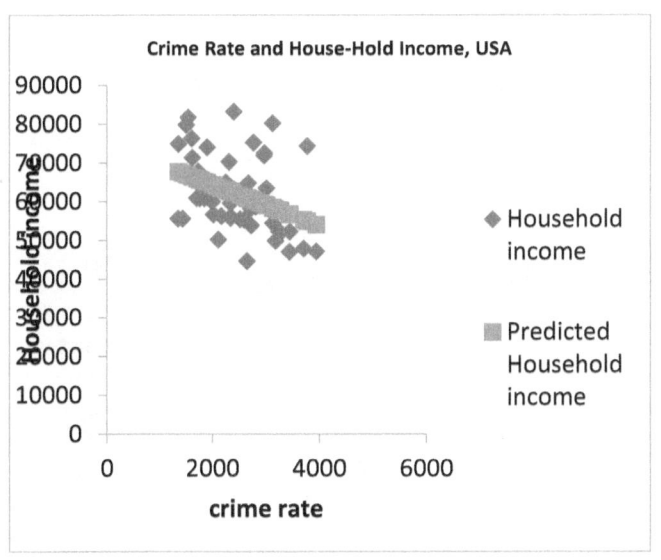

Rule of Law and House-Hold Income in OECD countries

Yet another example of OECD countries. Figure 2.4 tells us the same story. The rule of law is a causal variable for good income that translates into a good life. The question is how to live far away from the Deploville? The answer is simple: Rule of Law.

Figure 2.4

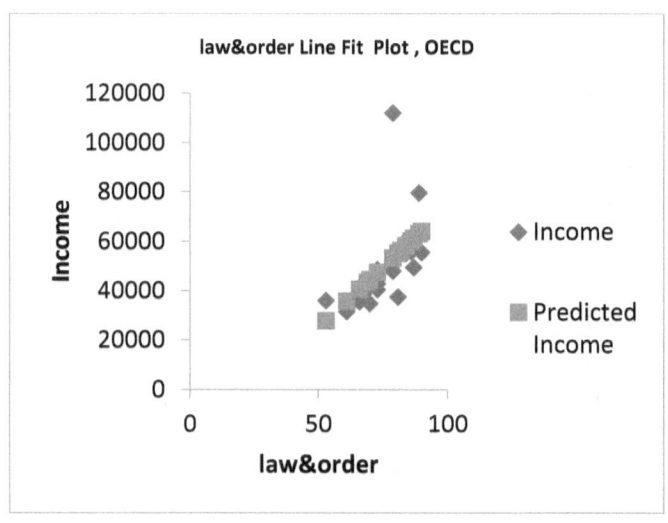

Ungoverned Spaces:

Ungoverned spaces are the spaces left unattended. One wonders why Nature's generously and bounteously endowed spaces on earth like Kashmir, Northeast in India, are continuously under chaos, destruction and have inefficient outcomes. Even spaces like Nice and Paris became less safe. It bears a semblance of a failed state, much less protection and safety, and people aspire for. Recent memories (2020) tell us that in Haryana's state, too, ungoverned spaces emerged, leading to destruction and chaos. Leadership was seen nowhere. It was an everyday struggle for main street people to survive; there was a potential threat lurking to explode, and it was like living life under fear continuously.

According to the Bible, "You shall not move your neighbor's boundary mark, ..." Then why are boundaries broken every day, much less respected. Neighbors, friends, colleagues jump walls, kill, and molest; families and neighborhoods become dysfunctional and unsafe. One of the most probable explanations is that when external forces become guests of internal hosts, the highly likely outcome is destructive and destabilizing. In a highly healthy functional substrate – a nation, a state, a family, a neighborhood, predators look for inviting nourishing spaces to act upon the destructive goals. The first step on this nefarious journey of rogue creatures begins with boundaries. If there are no boundaries, it's a piece of cake, and if the boundaries are there, the plan is always for puncturing a hole to escape into the realm of rogue elements' dreams. Recent and recurrent happenings in India and around the world have generated a debate: "Is globalization somehow responsible for outcomes we face; do we need to have closed boundaries; who are the beneficiaries of open boundaries; who are the losers, and who are the gainers in an era of connected and interdependent regions and neighborhoods?" One thing is noticeably clear: there is a movement of people and goods and services in open boundaries. As a result, osmotic forces come into play. Concentration on one side is highly likely to break walls and permeate. Rogue elements, too, have a chance to pass through. However, trade has benefits; globalization provides opportunities. Interconnection and interdependence are the facts of life in the modern world. We cannot wish away friends, neighbors, and colleagues out of civilized existence.

In a confusing world, we should build bridges but have boundaries, too, not to let the rogue elements in; be watchful of ungoverned spaces. In the first place, let them not be created; second, if they exist, identify unwanted external forces and internal hosts, and then act with a killer's instinct. It's like cancer – a rogue cell needs to be exterminated: chemo and lethal radiation. Rogue elements are no good.

A mango tree on the roadside is less safe than a mango tree in the backyard. We have a mango tree in our house backyard and a tree in front of our house on the curbside. Every year we watch, despite equally good, even better flowering, the curbside mango tree hardly bears mangoes, one would expect. However, the backyard mango tree provides fruits even to fulfill the needs of our neighbors – we distribute among friends and neighbors. The question is, why? The answer is obvious: boundary. The backyard mango tree is within the house boundary; the curbside has no boundary; anyone would throw stones and destroy much before mango fruits are ready. A mango tree tragedy, the tragedy of commons, and the tragedy of ungoverned spaces. Safety lies in governing the ungoverned spaces.

Environment and Governance

Human societies need economic development to survive and thrive. However, with development come environmental problems that put human life at risk. The question is: can we not live in harmony with Nature? Past examples of Easter Island, Maya, and Anasazi collapse and Ethiopia famine of 1984-85 have a lesson for modern-day societies: if we damage our environment and political chiefs are busy competing for self-interests, civilizations would be at risk. The civilizations of Maya and Anasazi were not wiped out because of external forces: external enemy or disease. Instead, these civilizations collapsed because of man-made conditions consistent with the destruction of the environment. According to Jared diamond, big businesses harm people by degrading the environment and imposing externalities in today's globalized society. It puts sustainable development at risk.

Life is a beautiful gift of Nature. One comes across beautiful people in this journey: just one nudge; just one brief encounter; just a sight; just one audience; just walking past by a door; just one smile; just one whiff of fresh air; just one great learning, makes one's life meaningful, bright, and exciting. Memories thus stuck in the hippocampus, algorithmically, keep life afloat. The substrate we grow in etches the rules of living. Some are born with an address, some work for it; some have the power to live free, some rise for it; some have access to pollution-free air and water, and some bear its burden. Who are these lives who still have no voice to free themselves from the clouds of bad air? And the government seems to care less.

This is about a place called "Mahul," in Mumbai, India. A separate set of rules seems to be applicable for these people. This is a case of people being thrown (rehabilitation) into the living hell of toxic air and contaminated water. Why these people did agree to shift to this place, one wonders. Simple: information deficit. But what about the environmental authorities who allowed clearances for such projects without safety measures? What about the elected representatives of these places – why did they not become their voice for pollution-free living? Are these the curses of capitalism and modern-day democratic institutions? Inequality generated by capitalistic approaches makes it more possible to shift the pollution burden on the less equal people. When power and wealth get concentrated in a few hands, two sets of rules kick in: one for the equals and one for the not-so equals. Research after research has indicated injustice rendered to the lower strata people. And adequate information does exist with the environment control authorities about the ground realities. The rule of law is a necessary condition to stop the toxicity of living spaces. We all are people, and inequality serves no one; pollution serves no one. Pollution-free living is a fundamental right of every person. However, in practice, even for breathing in fresh air requires credentials: haves vs have-nots bear different costs; scale tilted in favor of the rich.

What Do We Do?

We often hear from the state actors, none other than the Secretaries to the government (state government and federal government): "Forest is a mafia; Education is a mafia; Coal is a mafia; Mining is a mafia; Real estate is a mafia; Health is a mafia et al." question is: if the state actors cannot break these mafias, then who? I used to hear these words during my training at Mussoorie; I still hear these words from the retired colleagues after 35 years of job. Nothing seems to have changed. Lot has changed, though: inequality has increased, and mafias seem to have become more powerful and subtle. The fear of Socrates is still alive: to navigate a ship, a captain should be the one who should have the maritime and marine knowledge; if we choose a captain bereft of understanding, the sinking ship is almost guaranteed. Socrates believed in democracy; at the same time, however, he trusted thinking people for providing leadership; and no wonder he drank poison for the pursuit of education and knowledge – logic fired knowledge. Demagoguery is more prevalent in modern-day democracies because thinking persons do not seem to get a chance to be there, or they seem not to be participating in the democratic processes to avoid the heat and dust of election season. People get this chance once in four years, and if they choose the sweet shop owner, who makes people sicker by distributing freebies as against the rough and tumble of the expert person, who, like a doctor, would administer a painful procedure to provide a cure for the sickness, would it be an excellent choice? Certainly not.

Socrates was a thinking person and stood for the right thing, was punished; Christ stood for the right course, was put on cross; Gandhi Ji stood for the ordinary person, was shot dead; Luther Martin King stood for the civil rights and liberties, was shot dead, too. And after their departure, we worship them all: maybe, the collective brain of the masses is not wired to think fast enough. Or Socrates' advice for choosing a thinking person to lead has become a casualty even in modern times for personal gains. Inequality in society speaks volumes.

In India, there are concerns about the rule of law (2021) and crumbling governance. NN Vohra's report is still quoted as a window into the rot inside the administrative structure. Julio Ribeiro, an accomplished police officer (DGP – top police officer), keeps reminding people that all is not well through his write-ups. The recent (2021) Mumbai episode (though not much different from earlier episodes told by NN Vohra, the then Home Secretary) has brought turbulence to the public domain. The state actors, who are entrusted with the safety of life and property of the people, intrigued, designed, and crafted the dangerous scheme of money extraction from the tiny people owning small businesses by abusing the law machinery of the state to collect tributes from the humble people who eke out a bare survival level income from their small businesses. This bears a semblance of tribalism in a city known for the financial capital of a large country, India.

The question, however, is that we have been talking about this rotten stuff for a long time. We are repeating it almost every year in one report or another. For instance, in addition to NN Vohra's account and Julio Ribeiro's telling the truth, another book by Vinod Rai, an accountant of repute, speaks about the same rotten stuff and crumbling governance. Recent election (2021) commissioner's role has only added to the fuel. NN Vohra's call for refurbishing the old, rusted steel frame (Civil Services) seems to be in order. The danger to the steel frame is the rust within. How to take the rust off, there are a million options. The strategy lies in learning from the tried, tested, and well-understood natural laws (natural physical systems) of the physical world and apply them to the social systems of existence and governance. The analysis offers insights, and solutions are within reach.

For leadership of the day to see its people prosper, focusing on the rule of law is necessary. Justice, freedom, and the existence of independent democratic institutions are the requirements for democracies to thrive. Good law-and-order means the complete presence of the rule of law and the complete absence of corruption, cronyism, and nepotism. Lawful governance is consistent with outstanding leadership. Authentic leaders obsessively, compulsively, and consistently care for the safety of their people. Peace and prosperity often are the outcome. Without any doubt, the safety of the people is part of the economic equation, and the economy is a part of the life equation. The leadership of the day has no choice but to make law and order priority number one. Therefore, the significance of the "Rule of Law" parameter in the governance and leadership equation is high. Its absence brings misery, its presence spawns growth. It's not subjective; it's not an opinion; it is a scientific thing. The empirical data has a clear-cut pattern, which tells the tale.

An Example of UP (State in India)

In the state of UP, the CM, Yogi, clearly communicated to his officers the goal of improving the bad law and order in the state. For the years 2016-2021, crime rates went down by ~60%. Per capita income increased from 47000 to 94,000 in Indian Rupees. This specific case is a testimony to validating the hypothesis that law and order is a necessary condition for economic growth. Figure 2.5 says it all.

Figure 2.5

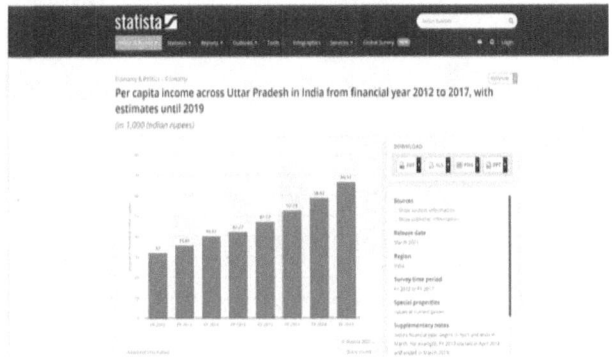

However, this improvement is comparative to previous years and not indicative of the fact that the rule of law in the UP is now up to the Gold standards of a democratic setup. People still have issues with the rule of law: treason cases against peaceful protestors aren't consistent with the rule of law. There are other issues as well. Politically connected people matter over the common people and opposition political party members' voice is suppressed. In this specific case of UP province what is evident, though, is that improvement in law and order has resulted in an uptick in income levels. Safe travel, especially during the night, and safe neighborhoods speak about the improved rule of law evidence. According to Julio Ribeiro, in one of his writings in a newspaper (the Tribune, September 2021), there is enough evidence that political and bureaucratic level corruption diminished during the regime of Yogi. The point is: if leadership is authentically authentic and plans for an improvement in the rule of law, it shows up in the income levels of the people. Lawful governance helps economic growth.

****

3

Be There

According to John Quincy Adams, "If your actions inspire others to dream more, learn more, do more and become more, you are a leader." Winston Churchill did not care for the bullets and visited his troops in the trenches; Chancellor Gerhard Schroder was trailing in his election, the flood came, and he was standing with the people in water; a mayor's popularity was slipping in New York, 9/11 event happened, he was there with the firemen helping people midst of hazardous debris; Democrats were struggling, Sandy Storm came, President Obama was seen in New Jersey. Being there helped both the people as well as the leaders. State actors got to be with the people in these uncertain times. Sitting in self-isolation is not consistent with leadership. Trump sulked in isolation after his defeat in elections; people suffered. Giuliani, the favored person of 9/11, too, joined the nefarious schemes of Trump and both became an embarrassment to the USA. They were just not there for the people.

Accessibility is one of the critical traits of an authentic leader. Accessibility means being there with the people to solve their problems. It means physically being there; it's about being transparent and having a conversation with people with an open heart. For instance, during a pandemic, in India, people were not informed what the government's intentions were, and decisions were taken closed door. The outcome wasn't efficient: migrant workers were thrown out of their workplaces and living places. It ended up in lots of pain, misery, and distrust between the people and the state actors/leaders. In the USA, too, transparency was missing; information consistent with leaders' political expediency was released. The outcome, again, wasn't efficient.

It's an attitude about welcoming people and interacting to know issues; it's not about enjoying a position and playing golf while critical issues await presence. It's about having a valid open-door policy; it's about management by walking around; it's about reaching out to them. The story happens at the place of its happening. Being at the spot offers an opportunity to know things firsthand, leading to an efficient evaluation of a situation and potentially the best workable solutions. Trust between the people and the leader is the foundation. Promoting a great relationship with the people and promoting the right vision helps people find their success. Being there means it's about people like parents are there for their family members. According to President Bush, "faith, friends, and family are a necessary condition for success." He also favored humility for authentic leadership – be there. "I must follow the people. Am I not their leader?" – Benjamin Disraeli. It simply means a true leader cares for the people and the concerns they have. As I am writing this page, farmers protest against lands laws in India has attracted the world's attention. Unfortunately, the state actors aren't caring for their concerns. Playing tricks with the good people the farmers are, has become fashionable with the state actors. The strategy seems to be tiring them and creating situations that would break their protest and ignore their concerns. This is not leadership; it's toxic. Good leaders put people first; personal ego and status are obstructive and inefficient for the proper outcomes.

"Bye, Pa!" Two words still ring in my ears, as live as then. It was 2001. Vikrant had a first parent meeting day just a week after he enrolled in the boarding school at Sanawar, class five. I paid deficient attention to the school calendar (schedule), especially about the parent-teacher meeting days: maybe there was no such thing during my school days in a rural setting; unconsciously, I overlooked it. Then there was this call: the phone rang, and I heard a low-sounding voice from my kid; he never sounded so low. He braved his tears, though. "When are you reaching? All other parents have reached here", he commanded. "Oh, my God! I am on my way," I lied. "Take a U-turn and drive fast as you can to reach Sanawar," I requested the driver. A moment of silence, and then the driver asked if everything okay. "How could I do it; how could I forget it?" I was preoccupied with my struggling mind without answering him. Such was the intensity of the mistake that would have imprinted on the kid's brain for the rest of his life. I missed on my coveted principle of leading by two words: "Be There." And I wasn't. However, I made it, little late, though.

Parents were sitting with their kids all around the school campus, and Vikrant Malik was looking toward the road for the car he recognized. I ran, and we did the drill we were used to, and I said, "I am so sorry." His confidence emerged, and he looked great. Well, then we roamed around a bit, and he spoke, and I heard. I decided to stay late to compensate for my missed timing. The final moment showed up: we both met the teacher and exchanged pleasantries. She was happy; we were pleased: "Okay, Mr. Singh, now you can leave; it's roll call time," she said. I looked at my kid and expected the drill I was used to at home – he would come running and jump to my shoulders for a bear hug. But this time, rules had gone under the transformation: he looked at me, raised his hand, and said, "Bye Pa!" It took a moment before I could settle down and fathom the reality that bear hug at school might not be consistent with peer living. "Yes, he is grown up now; yes, he is independent," I thought. I looked back again, and a little lost and less steady on my feet, he was gone with his school friends. Found my car, still preoccupied, and the driver again inquired, "Sahib, is everything alright?". I said, "Yes, let's drive back home." Two-hour journey, just finished in a flash and I was home still struggling, "Is he gone forever; no more time with him?" Two words still follow me, "Bye Pa!" Maybe, as a parent, I never wanted my child to go away. The reality, however, is different: life is a biological cycle – there is a beginning; there is an ending. The critical point, though, is: "Be There." Had I missed the day, it would have been a lose-lose game for both of us: I would have failed in my instincts; he would have carried the burden of left alone. In my case, it worked okay; in other absentee cases, I wonder how children cope with it.

"I Matrix"

Be the leadership at home or be the leadership at the workplace; the essence of two words always wins: "Be There." Moments, however, do come when opposing forces show up pulling in opposite directions between two words: "impulse and wisdom." The answer lies in the right choice. Do the right thing. Focus on the outcome. This is what wise people do. In the real world, people find it difficult to change, though. They choose to justify their actions instead of changing their behavior. Some people fall in the definition of stupid: knowing the truth, knowing the facts, still believing the lies. There are ignorant people, ignorant of their ignorance. For such people, it's a Freudian challenge to get at the bottom of the unconscious and bring it to the fore to resolve the conflicting minds. There is always a solution to each problem. Being there is the right thing to do.

We can use framework tools to know the right thing and then solve problems. One of the frameworks is "I Matrix," which has 'instinct' (impulse) on one axis and 'intelligence' (wisdom) on the second axis. The scale runs from low to high. For instance, high on instinct would translate human actions into genetic dispositions, which people genetically inherit, like instincts for survival. But Homo sapiens have evolved over the years, they live and thrive in civil societies. Learned behavior plays a significant role. Intelligence acquired over years of learning and experience does matter in leading a meaningful life. According to the Oxford dictionary definition of instinct is: "An innate, typically fixed pattern of behavior in animals in response to certain stimuli,"; and the meaning of intelligence is "The ability to acquire and apply knowledge and skills." Knowledge and skills acquired by humans do have a chance of solving problems arising out of innate instinctive tendencies. Following the framework of the "I Matrix," which is a tool to uncover the unconscious, we can pause a little and do CBA (cost-benefit analysis), not necessarily in dollar terms. As a consequence, a victory over raw instincts is highly probable. According to this framework, there are four types of persons.

First, **Dumb Lambs**; these are the people who score exceptionally low both on the instinct and intelligence scale. These people are ignorant: reasons could be defective genetic dispositions, or they might have missed the knowledge and skill train because of adversarial community substrates. Well, whatever the reason, the outcome is no good. The only hope for these people is someone takes care of them.

Second, **Pigs:** hedonistic lifestyle is the choice of many. They are high on instinctive living; animal spirits overtake the other concerns. Such people can be overly aggressive and pleasure-seeking at the cost of others. Knowledge and skill exposure might help such people.

The third type of people are **Toxic,** narcissistic and psychopaths. Such people are high on intelligence but low on empathy. They intellectualize everything around them. They refuse to change; rather choose to justify their behavior with one excuse or another. Their 'self' is at the center of their life: inflated self-image, high on ego, destructive, manipulative, and consider other human beings as objects to be used to their advantage. These people can only be helped by getting their unconscious to the fore.

The fourth category, which I admire, is the people who score high on both scales. These people are **Leaders** in the true sense of the word and help the world become a better place. Follow them, trust them. End of the day, what matters is not your wealth but "Who You Are." Toxicity hardly solves problems; authentic leadership does. These are the leaders who have the knowledge and are not ignorant of their own ignorance. These leaders are transparent in communication and consider the views expressed by the team members. They are inquiry-driven and do not give directions. They lead through a free exchange of views. For example, Toyota leadership model is highly appreciated. They use Bottom-up approach. In other words, employee engagement is high. Collective ownership of decision making is wider. Information flow is optimized.

I MATRIX

Instinct High   High, High

Pigs: Aggressive, hedonistic, Irrational, animal drives.	Authentic Leader: Cool, empathetic, humility, protective, **"know thyself"** the holy grail for them, neoteny, joie de vivre. Accessible and transparent.
Dumb Lambs, Innocent, Ignorant.	**Toxic Leader**: Robotic, high on calculus, inflated self, manipulative, low on empathy, justify their actions, blame others, fragile within. Destructive.

Low, Low   **Intelligence**   High

There are occasions when tough decisions need to be taken, and leaders do so. Decisions require mental clarity, emotional balance, vision, and courage. How a leader passes through these tough times can be self-painful and depressing at times. To keep a balance at such times, self-compassion, not self-criticism, is a promising idea. The very fact of life lies in its existence, and at times we got to adapt to tricky situations and not give up under even enormous pressure. Leaders do have responsibility and accountability and carry the burden home in isolation. According to research at Harvard Business School, leaders are likely to be 30% less stressed than the employees, the people they lead. With this self-knowledge, a leader got to be more mindful of subordinates and their pressure of coworking. This awareness only adds to the fact that it's leadership burden to be there for the employees as they are more likely to be under stress. If people are miserable, then trust and cooperation evaporate. The visioned path is lost. For instance, leaders enjoy the security of a job, status, and security. Leaders/CEOs/IAS officers have less to worry. But employees/subordinates may not be so lucky. Job insecurity, low wages add to their financial anxieties. The success of a leader lies in ensuring the well-being of the people they lead. They are there for them.

The challenge lies in providing a safe and secure environment to the employees for higher achievement. Providing certainty and clarity helps; it reduces anxiety. It's not uncommon for the state actors to show no concern. Slighting others, humiliating employees during meetings is quite common. Does it help results? The argument often put forward is "Danda (rod) Only Works" (intimidation brings about better results). However, researchers have shown, again and again, it's a short-term view. In the long run, outcomes are inefficient. According to, theory 'X' and theory 'Y' narrative, treating people with fairness, support and gratitude is superior leadership to intimidation style. Genuine and authentic leadership requires "Be Aware," "Be There," "Be Fair," and "Be Authentic."

****

4

Dignity of Work

A leader's strength lies in the people he or she is surrounded by. Selection of team, without any doubt, is critical to the task to be accomplished. Leadership is teamwork. As of today (2020), at this moment, COVID -19 has brought home that front line workers are the key-value creators. The dignity of labor could never have been more relevant. Whatever the job is, whatever the work is, people make it possible to happen. The point is simple: a great leader identifies and recognizes each team member down or up the ladder to be worthy of human dignity. It would not be out of place here to mention that the golden ratio rule should be applied to compensation. In today's world of capitalism (shareholders value creation seems to be the only goal), all is not good: a frontline worker is the lowest paid in ratio terms of value creation. We need to change the definition of capitalism as "shareholders' value creation" to the meaning of capitalism as "stakeholders' value creation." In this scenario, the goal would be fair compensation to all (top, down – golden ratio rule. Elitism is toxic), respect for the environment, and fair competition.

According to MIT research, "Dignity broadly refers to the recognition that human beings possess intrinsic value, are endowed with certain rights, and deserve respect." It further adds that individuals are worthy of respect irrespective of their status. By making employee dignity at the core makes strategic sense for an organization and leadership for efficient outcomes. Treating employees like objects is not desirable. According to this research, treating employees with dignity is an excellent way to walk the talk. In government organizations and agencies, during the meetings data is used for the evaluation of the projects and the performance of the employees working on these projects. Name them, shame them, approach is often used with a view for better performance next time. However, it involves human beings and treating them as subalterns is not consistent with good governance meaning thereby their performance cannot be expected to increase next time. Theory X has evidenced that treating employees as human beings only helps.

According to Harvard Professor Michael Sandler (Tyranny of Merit), "Is it a clever idea to make a college degree as an arbiter of merit?" Does it make sense that degree holders are superior and successful people and non-degree holders are losers and inferiors? Is success the sole contribution of the holder? So many elements seem to have been ignored traditionally: Contributors to the success of anyone individual include parents, happenstance, friends and buddies, family, and, of course, learning substrate – schools. Is their success, a doing of their own and alone? Does it corrupt the common good? According to Michael Sandler, it does. Meritocracy is corrosive and brings about hubris. Not equal opportunities exist for all. The top 1% income group of people send their kids to Harvard, more students than the bottom half of the population on the income scale. Circumstances are generous to the winners and oppressive to the losers. Only 1.5 to 2% of the low-income group reach the top earners' level even with college degrees. The winners and losers divide leads to rancorous tensions in society. No, it's not a correct picture. Martin Luther King said, "garbage pickers are no less-human beings, and their work is as important as of a physician."

The current Pandemic has shattered the illusion of control and certainty. The work of the frontline people has shown us that they are the saviors. Bottom line: Hubris of merit is invalid; in fact, inequality instilled by this class of people is harmful to many and to themselves. Every work is an equally important link in the chain: one link gone; the chain becomes dysfunctional. The tyranny is that the people on the frontline are not the best-paid people – nurses, truckers, grocery store clerks, et al. During this Pandemic, however, we see them as essential workers. Without them, the world would stop. Isn't it the time to reallocate income resources and ask a question to the "so-called" merit holders? Do CEOs deserve the wages they pay themselves? Isn't it time to look within and trust the golden ratio (Fibonacci series)? It is time to trust in science: high potential difference brings about sparks, high waters always flow to low levels until an equilibrium is reached. Yes, it's time for the proper equilibrium. If history is any guide, tensions build if the resources are allocated greedily and inefficiently in favor of a few (say, 10% VS 90%). Glorious revolution, French revolution, Arab Springs et al. are the natural outcome.

Memory is pretty fresh in my mind when I just joined a district posting and was responsible for various tasks, including law and order. It was just three days after I heard an officer, next in the rank, running breathlessly, and telling me, "Sir, it won't work." I asked, "What won't work?" I really thought, so new to the position, I might have screwed up. He said, "Sir, you address the class four employees as "Ji." They don't deserve it; it wouldn't go well with them, and work would suffer." He further added, "Just be rough and tough ('tar-phar,' the Hindi word he used) with them if you want them to be of any use." I felt relieved and thought, "I was okay." It was my turn now. After a brief pause, I asked him, "you, too, are my subordinate. Do you expect me to use the same disposition to take the best out of you?" Silence filled the room. I took this opportunity to explain to him the value of scientific research: Theory X and Theory Y. No concern was ever heard back. I kept respecting the duo and trust me, we performed well. The point is: class four, or class one, shouldn't find a place while dealing with people. All are special. A good leader recognizes this.

Inequality and Underpaid workers

Underpaying workers and living a parasitic life of luxury can't be a standard way of living; it must be full of psychopathic undertones. Isn't the leadership responsible for such a situation? Oxfam report January 2020 reveals in crystal clear terms that people are not justly and rightly compensated for their work that helps the generation of wealth for the economies around the globe. The wealth gap is so wildly wide that it does not make sense: concentration of wealth in just a few hands. **According to this report, the top 2153 rich people have more wealth than 4.6 billion people worldwide. Isn't it crazy? This report further highlights that women and poverty-stricken people work incredibly long hours a day and still survive in poverty-level wages. Their contribution to the economies seems to have been stolen by a few. Does it make sense to sleep on gold beds or use gold bathroom vanities? For these kinds of people, more is never more enough. Psychologists and psychiatrists would term it psychopath's delight. This certainly isn't right if history is any guide. Concentration in few hands is inefficient and inconsistent with authentic leadership.**

Figures for India are stark and tell even a deeper story of enormous inequality. One person's wealth increased in the year 2020 (a year of Pandemic where workers were thrown out of their jobs and were forced to the brutality of the authoritarian state actors, even forced to be sprayed with toxic chemicals) so much that it would be sufficient to keep 400 million poor people above poverty levels. Such is the enormity of inequality. If the state leadership is not responsible for it, then who? Isn't it toxic? The wealth of Indian billionaires increased by 35%, and millions lost jobs and were left to forage for food. Poverty increased, and the insensitive state actors inflicted the pain. Labor deserves dignity and their fair share in the wealth they contribute to creating in a nation. That's possible only if exemplary leadership exists. Less than 4% of rural households have computers, with a predominantly rural population in India. Less than 15% have an internet connection in rural India. Education facilities and health facilities are nowhere near to be called fair.

'Management by Chaos' seems to be the apparent lodestar of the seating governments to run its administration. Who benefits from chaos? Obviously, who intends to create it (Many political heads and the corporates are the clear-cut beneficiaries). Inequalities have increased, and rich have become more affluent, and the poor remain at the fringe. Indicators couldn't be louder: stock markets touched sky high, and economy touched bottoms – long lines of free food seekers in a country they call the richest. The capitalization of markets to GDP ratio hit a record high – 194% (good is 75%to 90%). Look at Tesla's stock value: PE ratio is more than 1700 (historical good PE ratio is 10 to 15). What kind of insanity has been generated by a few manipulators? Look at the wages paid to the frontline employees VS the ratio of the wages paid to the top seating heads: 1 to 300, 500, 1000, in fact, no limit (good is 1 to 10, 20, or even 30). Look at who gets the subsidies: the state actors give corporates like Amazon lands and tax breaks. The argument put forward is they create more employment. Really? What about the loss of jobs by retail and small businesses closing? Job loss data speaks volumes. Who pays taxes: rich or the other side?

My simple point here is: inequalities have increased, and it is against nature's laws of flowing water from higher gradient to lower gradient; power current flowing from the higher potential to lower potential; heat flowing from higher temperatures to lower temperatures, then, why the heck on earth, power and wealth keeps flowing towards the already rich? It's not a good sign: the day of reckoning would visit us, and there would be a meltdown. Democracy and an equal society are in everybody's interest. It's not rocket science not to figure it out. They say, "Nature is Beautiful." Yes, it's beautiful because of divine proportions: the golden ratio – 1.618. Yes, in nature, the golden ratio is 1 to 1.618. I think nature and science are a big deal; following it sure is in humanity's self-interest. The very idea of "Management by Chaos" is unscientific and against nature's laws. A golden ratio that we observe in nature's beautiful world would be a promising idea for the frontline workers and the people at the leadership positions to make a better world and equal universe. It would reduce inequality, and chances of upward mobility would increase. Compared to the USA and India, upward social mobility is much higher in Canada and EU countries. Denmark is an example.

It was 1986. I visited a doctor friend's place on the seventh floor of a multi-rising building in Mumbai (Bombay, then). Over a drink, we walked onto his balcony that overlooked Dharavi shanty area. He said, "You know, Mr. Singh, after some years, these shanty dwellers would be here, and I would be there." "There couldn't be a better statement of inequality," I said to myself. People down there lived in filthy dwellings leading a miserable life, and equally troubling was subconscious fear (of an uprising against the rich) on the gated community high floors. Did shanty guys move up (social mobility if you will)? The answer is: no. Inequality has increased, and recently, during the Pandemic, migrant workers had to run away back to their village homes. More misery descended upon them.

The income gap between the top and the bottom quartiles of the population has never been so big. According to 'World Inequality Report 2018', inequality has increased in India, China, Russia, and North America. According to this report, inequality has risen rapidly for the top 1%, and the bottom 20% of people's share has decreased rapidly. "While the top 1% income share was close to 10% in both regions in 1980, it rose only slightly to 12% in 2016 in Western Europe while it shot up to 20% in the United States. Meanwhile, in the United States, the bottom 50% income share decreased from more than 20% in 1980 to 13% in 2016." The report further adds that, at the same time, for Europe, there has been moderate inequality. According to an IMF (2015- study), the concentration of wealth in the hands of the top 20% of people is no good. "If the income share of the top 20% (the rich) increases, then GDP growth declines over the medium term, suggesting that the benefits do not trickle down". In comparison, "an increase in the income share of the bottom 20% (the poor) is associated with higher GDP growth."

The spiky and steep Lorenz curve speaks a lot about the prevailing inequality in the world. Corporates are wealthy enough to equal or exceed the total wealth of many nations. CEOs are rich sufficient to exceed the total wealth of their employees. Landlords own real estate enough to exceed the wealth of living tenants, and still, the story of unequal wealth/income distribution is as old as the story of potlatches. Affordable housing in India (even in developed economies) remains a dream for most of its residents. However, Gated community living is trendy for upper-middle-class people. Whenever elections are around, affordable housing is promised, and promises remain promises till the next election. Why are a few individuals have so much cargo, and many live by the fringes?

Wealth is generated by two factors: capital or skill. Many seem to be bereft of each, and few have both, at least one. If we take the instances of DHL, Amazon, Apple, Microsoft, et al., to begin with, all started with great skill and gathered wealth, the envy of many nations. However, their generations are born with a gold spoon – Reliance, Tata & Sons, DLF, etc. Also, CEOs of many corporations gather tons of wealth. The question is: why a CEO is paid in an asymmetric proportion at the cost of the workers at the cutting edge. The example of employees at Amazon, Wall-Mart et al., are instances of low wages. In countries like Bangladesh and other similarly placed countries, workers are exploited to the hilt.

According to Paul Krugman, Americans think upward social mobility is higher; however, the facts are otherwise. There is a crystal clear perceptual and reality gap when it comes to moving upward in terms of opportunities in the USA – The USA dreamland. According to Paul Krugman, "The key observation, based on a growing body of research, is that when it comes to upward social mobility, the U.S. is truly exceptional — that is, it performs exceptionally badly. Americans whose parents have low incomes are more likely to have low incomes themselves and less likely to make it into the middle or upper class than their counterparts in other advanced countries. And those who are born affluent are, correspondingly, more likely to keep their status". He further writes in his column on inequality and social mobility, "Back to the "potential for upward mobility": Where do people from poor or modest backgrounds have the best chance of getting ahead? The answer is that Scandinavia leads the rankings, although Canada also does well. And here's the thing: The Nordic countries don't just have low inequality; they also have much bigger governments, much more extensive social safety nets, than we do. In other words, they have what Republicans denounce as "socialism" (it really isn't, but never mind). And the association between "socialism" and social mobility isn't an accident. On the contrary, it's exactly what you would expect".

In India (even other countries, too), people who live in gated communities depend upon people who live outside the walls for services: household service providers – sanitary services, kitchen services, maintenance, and many more – live there in shanties with limited means. Outcome: hygienic issues. One of the bureaucrats, with a receding hairline, who retired as a top government functionary and chose to live in a big house in Gurgaon said, "Mr. Singh, the moment I get up early in the morning and get ready to go for a walk, I see these people releasing in the open; it's a mess. Then he complained and whined, "Power is not dependable: appear and regularly disappear at irregular intervals." I further inquired, "What about the water, sir?" He said it does flow through the pipes, but I am not sure about the quality; anyway, I use it." I kept the pace on, "How is the air quality"? "Oh, these johnnies from the municipality always sweep, collect and burn." He further added, "I avoid driving as roads are so clogged. During the rain, sewer effluents and water from the skies flow all in one". Oh man, he is breathing in filthy air and not sure of water quality. It's because unequal people work for him and live in his neighborhood: the creation of the wealthy. Isn't the reduction in inequality is in the self-enlightened interest of the rich only? Isn't it a time to recognize the dignity of labor, and everyone deserves a fair share?

****

5

Be Aware

Uncertainty is the fact of life. The higher the people go on the leadership ladder, the more uncertainty they deal with. In the rubric of physics, uncertainty increases entropy and thus disorder. To reduce entropy, information is the key. Shared information, as against isolated systems, helps reduce uncertainty. Inquiry-driven leadership is what the people would want in such an environment to deal with uncertain future and disorder problems. Information is unraveled by asking the right questions. However, blind spots do exist and are seldom addressed. Hubris, for example, blocks a leaders' capacity to know the knowable. Leaders have got to lead themselves against the ignorance of their ignorance. If they know that they know that they don't know, leadership skills can be upgraded by understanding the blind spots. For instance, in India, according to NN Vohra, non-sharing of information among departments (CBI, IB, CVC, ED, Revenue, are siloes) dealing with vital security information, good governance suffers. Internal security is the key to people's safety, and safety is a part of the economic equation.

Homo sapiens, as against the Neanderthals, had always been, have been, and still are searching for truth: the truth of life, the truth of happiness; the truth of organized life; the truth of leadership. Socratic "Know Thyself" is as relevant now as then. Socrates emphasized the inquiry method to know the knowable. Understanding the knowable is the hard part. Rest is not difficult. Two words: 'Be Aware' is critical to leadership. The fact of the matter is that the awareness part is missing most of the time. We do stuff, and we don't even know why. We follow the unreal and keep chasing it.

For instance, why do we walk with hubris; why do we wear attitudes; why 'I' takes precedence over 'team'; why do we take pleasure in slighting others; why do we serve a person and not the rule of law - constitution; why do we pay least to the frontline workers; why do we not care for the scientific temper even written in our (Indian) constitution? Does ignorance of own ignorance solve problems? Of course, not. The fundamental essence of leadership is solving problems. We can solve problems efficiently only if we know the issues and understand the consequences. Actions have outcomes: consciously measured steps have efficient outcomes. The obvious question would be: why to be self-aware? Research has shown that it brings home clarity; it brings home confidence; it brings home leadership that solves problems and communicates effectively; it brings home prosperity. But what is awareness? According to the Cambridge dictionary, awareness is: "Knowledge that something exists or understanding of a situation." In the field of psychology and existentialism, it is understood to be consciousness. Inquiry-driven leadership has its genesis in the Socratic inquiry method. It focuses on a question-based approach. Asking better questions helps problem finding and solving. Inquiry-driven leadership breaks barriers to creative thinking.

Awareness is a keyword that appears in leadership literature. Unfortunately, self-awareness is not so common among leaders as many would assume to be so. Research done by Tasha Eurich reveals that accurate self-awareness is a rare quality. It further shows that experience and power usually are a firewall to self-awareness, and introspection may not always help know the true self. So, saying goes, there are four types of people: first, people who have the knowledge and have knowledge that they have knowledge; second, people who have the knowledge and have no knowledge that they have knowledge; third, people who have no knowledge and have knowledge that they have no knowledge; fourth, people who have no knowledge and have no knowledge that they have no knowledge. Well, leaders would fall in the first category of people. They have the capacities and capabilities of recognizing and seeing clearly 'the real' hidden in the plain sight from 'the unreal.'

In psychiatry, the definition of unreal extends to disassociated self–deficit of attention and deficit of cognition. It might be an outcome of a trauma subject would have undergone, and to avoid the deep emotional burden, the subject disassociates from the real world. Perception of reality gets stressed, and a person defines his or her world far away from the natural, real. What are brain mechanisms that are different in persons who view the unreal as real? Well, neuroscientists have used fMRI machines to deep look into amygdala regions of the brain. Forget not that the brain mapping hasn't been accomplished as yet. Whatever is known, so far, is the best guesswork by scientists and psychiatrists. Amygdala, indeed, plays a significant role in reshaping the unreal into the real world of people who are self-destructive and dangerous to others. Is it a mental illness, or is it an outcome of the radicalization of minds with incomplete information? How do we make the real seem real, and the unreal seem unreal? For instance, facts speak climate change is real. However, skeptics brush it aside as fake; people wish to seek strength in diversity, which is real; politicians divide people into caste/creed/color lines, which is unreal; Babas (godmen) are unreal, and people take them as real; psychopaths nurture grandiose, which is unreal; and righteousness is ignored/punished, which is real. The fundamental cognitive challenge lies in making real the real and unreal the unreal. Yes, the Socratic world of truth: "Know Thyself," the authentic self (The role of 'Scientific Method' hardly needs any emphasis for knowing stuff: Observation, Hypothesis, Experiment/validate/testing, Theory/conclusion are the steps). There are known, knowns; there are known unknowns, and there are unknown unknowns. Known, known is the easy part, and we can handle it. However, knowing the unknowns is the hard part. Once known, it becomes easy. First, we got to be aware of what we are dealing with.

Elements of Awareness:

It consists of two parts: Hardware and Software. Hardware includes "two gametes, one zygote," the human body (skeleton), brain anatomy, the perishability nature of the hardware. The software part includes all the algos written on the brain through observation, learning formal and informal, unique experiences. Great leaders surround themselves with good books and good people. It writes algos on the brain (100 billion neurons and glial cells – not fully mapped, though).

Know what you don't know. Identify it, know it, accept it – don't deny it. Only psychopaths with narcissistic dispositions tell lies, deny, and if caught, they defy. This kind of leadership is toxic. For instance, on Jan 6, 2021, the head of the state of the USA nearly destroyed democracy. The good part is that democratic institutions withstood the stress, and the day got saved. This is one glaring instance of strong democratic institutions relevant for a country to serve its people. Toxic leaders destroy these institutions for personal gains. However, other leaders serve these institutions and show the path forward. The awareness that countries with strong democratic institutions lead people to prosperity helps leaders be authentic.

Human beings are a product of the phenomenon of nature; they are nature's construction of evolutionary accumulated knowledge. To be aware, we got to start with the anatomy of frames and structures we live in –the human body: the conscious part and the unconscious part of it. The fears and fragilities of yesteryears of human evolution lie in food and shelter, and safety. This is how the max life function explains why people unconsciously keep on making piles of money and claim success. What is success after all? Is it more money, is it the collective max of life function, or is it about all the attention you get and become a celebrity? What leaders are made of – the traits; what leaders do; how do the leaders spend time; how do they get fired to accomplish something important, and what keeps them excited and inspired restlessly to identify and solve problems; do they do it consciously, or do they do it unconsciously driven by the max direction of the life's scientific model – the life equation; do they have free will; do they live the authentic, real life, or do they live the unreal real life? What is the truth that human beings keep on searching for? Do the leaders hide behind religious sermons, little believing in science, and find truth in creationism instead of evolutionary theory? These are the questions that need answers in the process of awareness.

And in the modern life of today, it is money that buys food and shelter. Money offers opportunities for freedom, security, and safety. Accumulation, greed, and fear are explainable from the equation of life (explained on the next page – what's life?). The accumulation phenomenon is unconscious, and the algos of fear and fragility have roots in the evolutionary process. In today's civilized world, where the capacity to know exists, the conscious as against unconscious becomes relevant. Self-awareness of humans helps to know the existence of life. Every life is equally vital in existential terms: no one is special, and if special, everyone is special – the special creation of nature. The raw nature of living must give way to the civilized and learned way of living. Nature's laws are loud and clear: we are born equally. Self-awareness of nature's life phenomenon helps in respecting all the lives.

Unmasking the Unreal:

We always wonder what we really are: our real side, and what is our blindside? The brain is a physical part.

According to dual theory, the brain and mind (consciousness) are two separate things. However, the mind cannot exist without the brain – the brain is a necessary condition for the consciousness of self and the world around us, but not a sufficient one. What is consciousness, then? It is hard to define – closest would-be awareness, and in physical terms, it has something to do with neurons: no neurons; no consciousness. This is what neuroscientists have found out from their clinical experiences and through fMRI images. Are human beings just a biological complex machine, or do they have free will? How do we make decisions? Does the biological machine autonomously make nerve-motor connections execute decisions and decisions? It just needs a stimulus to kick in. Well, what happens after it kicks in? Is it automatic, or is there free will (a set of options to choose from and then consciously decide to execute it, or not to execute it)? Free will means complete control of the machine we call it brain. How many times, we ask ourselves, maybe I would haven't done so? This takes us to the level of something that the brain does autonomously.

Aren't we on autopilot most of the time – we do stuff even we need not to? With progressing scientific research and tools being available, more and more information is piling on to know what we know. Neuroscientists are working on defining human behavior as a function of the brain as a physical-biological machine; however, each individual is unique in its connectome (brain's biome) and uniquely different. The Corpus callosum is a connecting part of the brain anatomy. The size and architecture of the wires connected within the brain define the connectome of an individual. That would be a broad understanding, and brain mapping is still in its infancy. Brain plasticity, the neurons, the glial cells, and now new information- hundreds of thousands of specialized cells exist within a brain – makes it still more complex. However, we can agree that each individual has his or her connectome unique to himself or herself. Knowing one's connectome is just like a Socratic "Know Thyself." Isn't it like going to a basement to switch on a tripped switch to bring the light back on? Yes, there is always a blindside within. Smart people know it and turn the right switch on and get back to life, to have a great run; stupid even don't know the subconscious and unconscious (basement of the brain, if you will) parts of their connectome. Yes, the connectome is a unique, complex, and comprehensive map of neuron pathways within a brain. I am my connectome;

you are your connectome. Know your connectome; know the blindside – life would be authentic.

'Know thyself, then, seems to be a key to orderly living. Never know, cool-looking guys might be carrying lots of burdens of unconsciousness and have the potential of harming themselves as well as people around them even without being aware of it. Socrates 'Know Thyself' is very much evidenced with the use of modern fMRI tools of science to be valid. As one steelmaker said, "Nobody can kill iron, but itself, from its rust." The most significant dangers lie deep buried within only – deep into the medial temporal lobe. Invoke upon your scientific skills to know yourself. "The two most **important days** in one's **life** are the **day** one is born, and the **day** one finds out why"– Mark Twain. Then, the logical outcome seems to be the "Know the 'Why' part. Know the truth; it will set you free: free of temptations, ignorance, falsehoods, lies, denials, personal gains/greed, fear, cognitive dissonance, and cognitive bias.

What's Life?

The goal of life is to lead a happy life. Goals are better defined.To be aware, we need to define life then. Without knowing the views of one of the greatest in scientific thought, Albert Einstein, the meaning of life won't be sufficient. According to him, life is a part of the universe in space and time. It simply means life is a moment in time. According to Erwin Schrodinger (Physicist, Nobel), life is negative entropy. We consume low entropy organisms and leave high entropy materials. In physicists' world, life is an isolated irreversible system, however, continuously interacting with its surroundings. The second law of thermodynamics and entropy find a place in understanding life's phenomenon. In the world of biology, life is a structure of information biological molecules-DNA. Life is a natural phenomenon and is a biological process inherently regulated with information hardcoded on the particles forming it. Acquired information (knowledge) adds to maximize its functions. Instinct and intelligence are the two ingredients that are the essence of life information networks. Working with instinct or with ignorance would bring about different outcomes than working with intelligence and knowledge. Knowing life with a perspective of information adds to the awareness process. People do stuff out of instinct and ignorance, and people do things with intelligence, design, intrigue, and intentions. Either way, most often, the outcome is dangerous.

Awareness offers an opportunity to avoid trouble. A leader's strength lies in knowing stuff.

In the rubric of physics, life is an ordered functional structure with low entropy. Albert's moment in time, Elvin's negative entropy, Shakespearian sound and fury, Darwin's evolutionary process and adaptive instincts, Paul's information-loaded life molecules all tell the story of life as a functional creature. Life's maxed function wraps it all. The equation of life is on the following page. This is a utility function and it's a utilitarian appraoch to comprehend life.

$$L(x) = A * f^\alpha * s^\beta * r^\gamma$$

Here 'f' is existence – food and shelter, 's' is safety (the rule of law), and 'r' is regenesis. Information molecules of life are hardcoded to maximize the living conditions, and thus, it goes on. Life adapts under changing conditions as it is coded to survive. If it fails to adapt, it's a goodbye – death.

The entire process of leadership is about the good life. To know "what's life" is critical for a leader. It would be a promising idea to be aware of what exactly life is about. Is it a biological machine or a special creation of some superpower we call God? The protagonists of evolutionary theory do not fall in line with creationism theory. To have faith in science is not a bad idea and the theory of evolution offers insights into the existence of life. According to existentialism, life is a hard reality, and individuals find themselves in a situation they are thrown into. Adaptation, then, only is the path forward. Let's then have a workable definition of life as existence, and life is a biological condition: two gametes, one zygote, and then multiplication of cells. Life is a moment in time: it begins and ends. Life span depends upon survival conditions: food and shelter, safety, and regenesis. If we understand the very basics of life, it helps us solve problems that are consistent with organized civil life. Humans are a life different from other lives because they have the capabilities of using and devising tools for use. Other lives do have abilities that humans don't have; however, every life is important for a biome's living and thriving, and recognizing this fact helps humans only. Recognition of keystone species is critical to an equilibrium existence. The ecosystem will be damaged if the keystone species disappear. For instance, bees are the keystone species: if bees disappear from the scene, plant life, and hence other lives dependent on plants, would fall in jeopardy zone. Being aware of keystone species, humans can help ecosystems from destruction.

The phenomenon of hating and stigmatizing people who have been treated for the virus is so unscientific. Out of their ignorance, people are invoking snake oil solutions; even some of the state actors left the migrants behind and spent money and precious time on disinfecting channels without any evidence, later on, to be abandoned after the scientists raised their voice. Why do we hate? It has no science genesis. The equation above has no variable that would suggest that hate would increase survival chances. Scientifically, hate reduces the life function value. According to this equation, hatred, jealousy, slighting others, and hubris, at best, are self-diminishing traits; at worst, it's a process of self-destruction. Put any positive value of these elements in the equation model, the life function's value goes down. And this is consistent with a Shakespearean view: "Out, out, brief candle! **Life's** but a walking shadow, A poor player that struts and frets his hour upon the stage, and then is heard no more: it is a tale told by an idiot, full of sound and fury, signifying nothing." Mahatma Gandhi said, "don't hate the sinner; hate the sin." This distillate idea of Gandhi Ji resonates with this equation. It is amazingly simple: hating a person diminishes function's value. Confrontation (Gandhi Ji preached Non-violence; it's so scientific), too, diminishes function's value.

"R" element, simply put, is knowing the existence, the essence of thrownness in nature. Life is nothing but nature's biological phenomenon, a process of living, beginning with two gametes and one zygote and ending with the ultimate truth of life – death. The more we know about it, the more we efficiently adapt to the facts of life and live it with dignity without undermining the dignity of others.

Life function is consistent with existentialism thought as well. This model can also be used as a tool to comprehend the essence of life and adapt to the circumstances an individual finds himself or herself thrown into. It helps understanding why we behave, the way we behave: each existence (individual) has its unique truth, and to live a life of inauthenticity (falsehoods, lies) leads to pathology. Pathology harms the carrier and the domino effect that troubles many others; the whole country suffers if a pathological person finds a place at the top. Existentialism school of thought is pro authenticity and uniqueness of each existence given the existence and then the attainment of essence (the character, traits, habits, behavior of an individual, among other things). Essence comes to an individual through observation, interactions with siblings and friends, learnings, and unique experiences.

Thus, becoming aware of the unique existence is a path forward to adapt to individual's unique substrate he or she finds entwined into. It's not that simple, though, to get it and become aware of the complex, dynamic, and arduous nature of existence. It's ongoing inquiry (Socratic inquiry, "Know Thyself" if you will) that surely helps. Authentic leaders are aware of people's problems, and they have the know-how to untangle problems. Not 'being aware' would be ignorance and leading from ignorance is dangerous. In democracies, demagogues, at times, find their way to the top. Ugly outcomes pop up, and people face the brutal realities of their life. Two words 'Be Aware," help not only the electors but also the elected. Leaders are the only ones who have the knowledge and have the knowledge that they have the knowledge. They are authentic leaders.

****

6

Hubris

Hubris manifests in a person when he or she displays extreme pride and extreme confidence. In the business world and the political world, unrealistic estimation of own professional capabilities would often be exhibited. Hubris represents an over-emphasis on self-accomplishments. It's visible in leaders, self-promoting by using words, "never before such an accomplishment was ever achieved." "Never before in the history of our country economy and stock prices increased to such heights; never before people respected our country abroad," head of a state often would say. Recent covid 19 surge and chaos in India speaks of Covid Hubris. It's a catastrophe; people are living in fear, virus spreading at a rapid speed. Indian leadership declared victory (April 2021) over the pandemic to find ground reality facing the false claims. Hubris makes a leader kiss dust. In the corridors of power civil servants in India are often heard saying, "It's for the first time we have accomplished this – every time, it becomes the first time, I have done it." For an authentic leader, credit goes to the team, however, in hubris laden environment, the leader is more concerned about self-promotion and credits himself or herself at the cost of team members.

Leadership characteristics that inspire people include charisma, charm, length, and breadth of vision, and leaders' respect. Successful leaders do seem to have sharp communication skills to connect with people and show confidence in dealing with demanding situations. However, there is a blind side to it that includes impulsivity, a self-assumed image of "Mr. Know all," firewalling communication from opponents, not listening to advice, and creating a wall between their world and the real world. Often, juniors have a great point to make, and seniors take no time to shoot it down. Politicians would very often ignore what they don't want to hear. Business leaders with hubris end up in failure. Hubris is perilous to the organizations managed by hubris-ridden leaders. This leads to inefficient outcomes.

The common thread that weaves across hubris includes arrogance, ignoring the evidence, false pride, heightened self, and contempt for others. According to the

Cambridge dictionary, hubris is: "an extreme and unreasonable feeling of pride and confidence in oneself." Hubris syndrome is a situation where a person's behavior suddenly changes to self-grandiose triggered by a power position. However, hubris-laden people fall back to remission in the absence of power – behavior changes and no longer consistent with grandiose.

Hubris is a communication firewall that dangerously destroys many successful leaders, and the cost is extremely high for the people affected by such leaders' decisions. They fly too close to the sun and end up in total meltdown: they fail themselves and let down the people they lead. As the drama unfolded in the USA for a transition (not peaceful, of course) on Jan 20, 2021, after the violence (failed coup) on Jan 6, 2021, from the previous leadership to the new democratically elected, everybody asked a question: who failed – leadership or the coup d'état. Comparing two leadership styles became obvious: one put people first; the other put the self (power position) first. Indeed, leadership failed for the simple reason that it was never about the people. Hubris was visible so transparently that the leader in position made best efforts to arm-twist people of right wisdom. Coup d'état, too, failed because strong leadership emerged at the level of democratic institutions. New leadership displayed humility over hubris in its actions immediately after taking over the driving seat. George Bush was once asked, "what is leadership?" He answered in a single word: "Humility." Yes, leadership is all about people and humility; hubris is anathematic. To lead people authentically requires one to have empathy, ethics, morality, and humility. Hubris has no utility value.

Is Hubris a Personality Disorder?

It's not very uncommon to see Babus (bureaucrats) and Bhai sahibs (politicians) swaggering around in the corridors of power – state actors' place of work. Babas (self-styled godmen), too, behave "divinely" and sit on high portals at the faith congregation places to instill awe and divine fears. Business leaders seem not to care for the front-line workers, and inequality keeps skyrocketing. In the current pandemic COVID 19 phenomenon of the bailout, big money appears to have served the wealthy better: rich became four times richer, and poor stood in long food queues. A large chunk of money, so doled out, found a place in the stock markets: real economy and unemployment showed cracks while the stock market kept increasing to all-time highs. Doled out money is taxpayer's money; the rich hardly pay taxes (tax cuts benefited the rich). The bailout money finds its place in the stock market to further rich the already rich, including politicians who are privy to the game of bailout. Doled out money did not find a place in the capital investment or manufacturing sector. Main street people pay twice: pay taxes, and then doled out money goes to the corporate world later to be recovered from them in the form of taxes. Rich seems to have loads of hubris and display wealth.

A sizable portion of such actors (leaders) seems to suffer from a hubris personality disorder in plain and simple words. And the people have got to live with it – the toxins of hubristic leadership. It's not uncommon to observe frightful walks of leadership in positions of power. The simple strategy they seem to work with is shock and awe; it's 'I' versus 'they' – subaltern if you will. Once by hook or by crook (by crook, most of the time) they are there, they seem to forget walking on mother earth; the pain of the main street people remains no longer their concern. Somehow 'H' factor (humility and honesty) of their persona evaporates till they again kiss dust. The Satan of hubris overtakes their brain. People with self-assumed arrogance, slighting others serve no one. However, hubristic decisions are bone breaking for ordinary people. Once these cool-looking guys sit on the throne of power, imagine what harm they can inflict upon. Hubristic decision making is characterized by impulsivity, confabulation, telling lies, non-empathetic responses, manipulative trickster, feeding on fears of others, heightened sense of self, contempt for others. This is not consistent with authentic leadership. It's rather an imbalanced personality.

Is hubris syndrome acquired disorder or genetics originated? Is hubris a mental malaise? Dictators with almost no constraints tend to have hubris. Instances of Hitler, Stalin, Mao, Saddam, et al. fall in the category of hubris. Saddam had even Bipolar (Owen 2008) personality disorder. The point is: is hubris a personality disorder? DSM V hasn't listed it as such so far. However, leadership with hubris means a complete absence of empathy and complete presence of heightened self and grandiose, caring little for people's concerns and complaints. 'H' factor absence in leadership spells out trouble for main street people. Hubristic leadership pulls a plug on reality; takes decisions anthemic to the lives of taxpayers. Leaders with hubris, walk-in power, exceed in madness, miss on the "H" (humility and honesty) factor, and make decisions for personal gains. Hubristic leadership, then, clearly falls into NPD (narcissistic personality disorder as per DSM 5) and, thus, a personality disorder. NPD people have the traits of pathological liars, absence of empathy, and presence of a heightened personal image. Power position offers them an opportunity to express these characteristics in excess and thus sure trouble for people they govern and for whom they make decisions.

President Trump suffered from this malaise, according to Harvard Professor Howard Gardener. According to him, "Trump is an easy case to diagnose as NPD case." The Professor did add that people with NPD (narcissistic personality disorder) become more so with increasing age. It is validated in President Trump's case. Democracy nearly fell into a death spiral of his last days – Jan 6, 2021. Till the last, he kept on insisting on the unreal facts of winning the election. "He's so classic that I'm archiving video clips of him to use in workshops because there's no better example of his characteristics," said clinical psychologist **George Simon,** who conducts lectures and seminars on manipulative behavior. "Otherwise, I would have had to hire actors and write vignettes. He's like a dream come true." According to psychotherapist **Charlotte Prozan,** Narcissism is an extreme defense against one's own fragility, insecurity, and feelings of worthlessness. To degrade people is part of a Cluster-B personality disorder: it's antisocial and shows a lack of remorse for other people. The way to make it O.K. to attack someone verbally, psychologically, or physically is to lower them." That's what he did in his presidency.

Persons with hubris disorder sitting at the top could be dangerous, and the ordinary person has no choice but to suffer the inflicted wounds (self-inflicted wounds in democracy by electing such people). Isn't it a great idea to be aware of such malaise and be an effective, authentic leader? According to Greek literature, hubris emerges from insecurity. In ancient Greece, 'hubris' is described as the behavior of an individual with power and leadership position who gets intoxicated with excessive pride, unfaltering self-belief, and overweening self-confidence. A person with hubris treats others with disregard, disrespect, and contempt. Power goes to the head of a hubristic leader to the extent that he or she misperceives, misinterprets, and misjudges the realities of the situation and makes severe and fatal errors of judgment.

The awful persona, however, seems to tumble down once the powder dries up; they seem so frightened, holding their tail between their legs. Haven't you seen state actors after retirement or after losing elections crying, at least complaining, and not vacating government housing? Hubris, thus, seems to be an acquired syndrome by people with inherent insecurity. If this is a personality disorder, isn't it a good idea to screen people for this disorder? Or, even for that matter, potential leaders must pass through a training capsule to make them aware of such missteps and then put them on personality tests that would rule out the syndrome. It's simple: hubristic decision-making is not efficient; decisions outcomes involving coordination, cooperation, humility, honesty, and integrity are efficient – the science of game theory. Hubris has the least possible benefits for good governance.

Tragedy of Hubris

Hubris is often followed by nemesis. Power, position, and status for a continuous period is a breeding ground for hubris. Intuition and gut feeling rule decision-making, and information is often ignored. It leads to failures and risky decision-making. According to researchers, two mechanisms bring about overconfidence and dangerous risk-taking behavior. They ignore the uncertainties of a situation and take an over-simplistic and optimistic view. Second, they overestimate their capabilities and capacities of problem-solving and overestimate the resources available. For instance, a head of a state said, "Virus would be gone soon." However, the facts proved him wrong again and again. It's what leaders with hubris do: don't want to listen against their false truths. His actions ended up in disastrous outcomes. Despite the best medical facilities in the USA, the virus killed the highest per capita in the world. People going hungry and standing in free food queues for hours in the wealthiest country of the world is unimaginable. A leader with hubris seemed to care less for the people than his personal gains. In India, too, Covid hubris was on display. In the business world, corporate-level hubris is infectious, and examples are numerous companies gone bust and bankrupt. The hubris of success breeds success leads to overreliance upon cognitive heuristics and intuition decision-making for much more complex and dynamic situations.

Leaders with celebrity status fall prey to a romantic, larger than life-size, the aura of a hero, the Invictus feeling, that starts running into their bloodstream. Straight from the gut, decision-making overlooks everything else. The outcome, obviously, rarely is good. Self-awareness and discernment are required, and good leaders aren't easily broken from reality. A psychologist would indulge in self-realization moments for a real leader. It would be correct to say that leaders overloaded with hubris are fake. Only authentic leaders are capable of leading and able to navigate the ship to shores. To keep in check the hubris of a CEO, a chairperson with a board is a necessity in the business world. The tendency of fusing CEO and chairperson role into one individual is perilous.

The tragedy is that leaders with intuition and managing by guts are praised and have positive connotations. In the political world, intuition is taken as the hallmark of good leadership. Gut feeling and intuition feeling for a correct move are considered as necessary as rational analysis. The thing is that humans are irrational, and they are angry if things don't fall their way. Neuroscience, through fMRI machines, has revealed a lot about how the decision-making process works. Neuroscientists have gone to the extent of suggesting that humans are not wired to think. Thinking involves looking at the alternatives available and then evaluating and then choosing the best. Leaders with hubris get buried into their own world of reality. They rely heavily on their own intuition – a feeling of doing the right thing and live in a bubble surrounded not by someone who projects honest, disinterested perspectives about what's real and how he might handle it. Great leaders, on the contrary, have this quality of surrounding themselves with good people who can call a spade a spade, and they appreciate that. However, leaders laden with hubris seldom appreciate and the real world is not always the world they define for themselves.

Hubris and Free Will

Is Hubris a hamartia, or leaders, laden with hubris, choose it as a deliberate strategy to govern? Is it fateful for a leader to be controlled by events despite their best intentioned acts? In other words, does fate control the outcome despite having a free will – choosing out of options. In Greek mythology, in Oedipus the King, fate and free will play a significant role in the destruction of Oedipus. According to neuroscientists, people are rarely conscious of their doings. Free will means: to be able to make decisions free of constraints. Well, let us try to have a workable definition of free will. Functionally, 'Free Will' has two components: first, absence of any force – constraints; second, presence of rationality. Oxford dictionary defines free will: "The power of acting without the constraint of necessity or fate; the ability to act at one's own discretion." However, according to Kane (2005), it's hard to define free will. Free will, indeed, is a brain function. Understanding brain functionality, therefore, is a good start. Can we understand brain structures and their functions by pushing people into fMRI machines and recording electrical impulses? Neuroscientists are doing it.

Should we understand the hubris then as a thing into the brain with an analogy of a computer machine that permeates our lives today because it deals with information and helps decision-making? It stores data; it slices and splices information to move on the device functional's instantiated objects of routines and subroutines. Lots are being accomplished in the field of AI (artificial intelligence). However, let's be clear that the human brain is a 'Brain' and certainly not a computer. The reason is straightforward: consciousness. Humans have consciousness, and computers don't have it. What is consciousness, though? Well, again, a workable – functional definition: consciousness is the integrated set of information drawn from the hippocampi and spliced and interpreted with the environmental clues – stimuli in the domain of awareness. It is the stream of information packets coherently ordered from the brain's memory repertoire activated as a consequence of stimuli received.

With a gift of consciousness, a brain is a biological machine that develops its routines and subroutines to make the machine work. Who writes these routine and subroutine codes? It's an experience that an individual goes through day after day, every day. The environment is critical, which is the second half of this machine that works on the first half – hardware, genetic existence, the hard code stuff. Hardware, thus, is a necessary condition for making and keeping this machine functional. Routines and subroutines may be likened to a capacity built up of skills and abilities to make decisions. However, these routines and subroutines are unique to every person depending upon the unique hardware (genetic dividend) and unique experiences, and unique environmental substrate. For instance, a person inflicted with psychological illness has no free will to make a decision of consequence. And leaders with hubris would take the organization to perilous outcomes.

What do neuroscientists say about free will? Some neuroscientists have been able to tell, based on their research, that decisions precede consciousness, and thus, free will is of no consequence. Meaning thereby free will does not exist. However, the fact of the matter is that still, there is no final word in the neuroscience world about the connections within neurons and glial cells. How 86 to 100 billion neurons with thousands of dendrites create connections and how many permanent and how many in the state of flux, aren't yet scientifically established. So far, computers don't exist to handle that kind of data. It is still a mystery to be unraveled. Brain mapping project is the hope. As of today, we can agree upon the fact that people do make decisions, and decisions are based upon the information. How this information is processed into a brain is unique to each person. Constraints, too, are a fact of living life. Given the level of the constraint, the freedom to take a decision gets diluted proportionately. It would be safe to say that the index of the constraint inversely affects free will. The question now is: how to diminish the constraint index? The answer is simple: "Kill Hubris."

Why 'free will' at all is a relevant point to be discussed and worked upon? The answer lies in the fact that humans are born with free will and wish to pursue their lives with free will. Democracies are the consequences of freedom people want to live with. However, freedom does have constraints so that one's freedom does not infringe upon other's space. This is a lifestyle far away from the domain of slavery, which human races faced in the past and are facing now in one shape or another. Constraints can be helpful and in favor of the free will. And restrictions can be imposed upon the self-serving interests of the rogue routines in the brains of devils. Is it something like good cholesterol – bad cholesterol narrative? Maybe. The fact of the matter is that free will is a goal, and constraints are a reality. Mathematically speaking, Free Will is an objective function and maximize the function subject to the constraints imposed upon by the routines embedded deep into the brain through a lengthy process of development in an environmental substrate unique to each person is the goal. "My Neuron – Myself" is a unique brain fingerprint of each person. Then why do we always tend to compare people and expect them to behave the way we wish them to? Wouldn't it be consistent with biological sciences to recognize differences and thrive in diversity? Tolerance level, in other words, empathy, is a brain function, which can be codified with environmental plasticity. Hubris has no scientific basis.

When psychopaths make decisions, it affects us all. As per one of the research data, psychopaths do trickle down to the ladder of public service architecture. The name of Hitler is awfully familiar. Again, natural scientists and their work come very handily: Hare Psychopathy Checklist offers an opportunity to figure out the psychopathy problem. The crucial point here is of empathy. How many state actors do indeed have empathy levels consistent with democratic values? CBI raids (2020) on the premises of erstwhile total government dispensation in the state of Haryana – Former CM Haryana, his former top officers, and other aides indicate an absence of it. It appears that they were there just to grab from the poor farmers their lands and conspire with the sharks of private builders. Isn't linear dispensation of nonlinear constructions an untruth? Isn't CD (cognitive – dissonance) resolution by pathological lies a disaster? The question is: do people do it out of design, consciously, or they do it because unknowns-knowns are deep buried into their subconscious? If they do it out of design, they are evil; and if they do it because of unknowns-knowns, there is something rotten and filthy in our constructions that need to be cracked, and the self-alienated need to come back to the authentic self for harmony and peace. Else, we do sure face a decline. If we are a nation of free will, recruiting process for keeping psychopaths away or making them aware of the ills of psychopathy that get routinized deep into our brains needs to be rewired through training and making the trainees aware of the brain functional outcomes. A little awareness of cognitive functions would bring self-insights and lots of empathy, the absence of which leads us toward psychopathy.

The truth is that people do make decisions, and decisions have consequences – sometimes expected, sometimes unexpected. Decisions of people make a difference in the lives of the people. For instance, why are some countries more developed, and others are not? It's certainly the outcome of decisions and conscious processes that precede in taking decisions. The neuroscience experiment shows doubts about free will because actions preceded before brain areas could activate. Routines and subroutines impact decision-making processes; however, a consciousness of routine and subroutines deep-buried into the hippocampi impacts the free will to make the right decisions to keep the same routines safe and keep the machine running. Hubris is an acquired syndrome, and triggers are the power, position, and status people have got by happenstances. Structures and frameworks help identify such people, and further damages to be inflicted by such people are avoidable. For instance, in democracies, there are checks and balances to deter lunatic decisions by hubris-filled leaders. This is possible only through a built-in mechanism of strong democratic institutions. If we know the knowns, it helps change the course and navigate a ship in the right direction. The vanishing of hubris helps both the people as well as the leadership. Evil of hubris is not fateful; it is an instance of free will. People choose it the way they behave.

****

7

Beatus Pursuit

Does GDP measure the well-being of a nation? This is the question that has been raised and answered by different experts differently. Richard Easterlin raised an empirical proposition of whether economic growth improves the human lot. According to Stiglitz, Nobel Laureate, emphasis on growth is misguided. There is more than GDP that should be the measure of wellbeing of the people. Research has shown that economic growth does help happiness; however, after a level, it plateaus. It behaves like a logistic function. There is a limit to the happiness a human can contain or capable of having it. Alternatively, the diminishing rate of return to increase in income plays a vital role. Empirical data suggest that despite income growth in real terms, happiness is more or less stagnant after some income level. Following graph, figure 7.1(screenshot), makes it clear that in the USA, despite income growth, human well-being did not increase in tune with the income increase.

Figure 7.1 (Screenshot, USA)

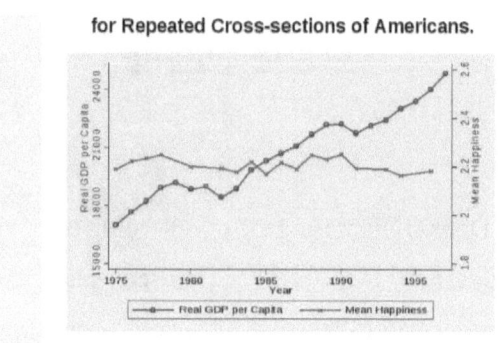

Similarly, the same pattern is visible in the case of Italy, Figure 7.2. It has been observed in the case of other countries that increasing per capita income helps people's well-being to a point, and then it flattens out.

Figure 7.2 (Screenshot, Italy)

According to AJ Oswald, fear depresses happiness. However, low levels of unemployment and low levels of inflation make people happy. Easterlin further adds that humans are concerned with relative position. Their happiness is referral. Individual's own income and other's income play a part. In other words, happiness is subjective.

People expect from a leader contented living conditions. For a great leader, then, to have an awareness of what's the science behind happiness makes sense. The narrative of happiness is as old as human history. According to Robert J. Shiller, the human brain has always been highly tuned towards narratives, whether factual or not, to justify ongoing actions. He further adds: Narratives go viral. So, what's the narrative of happiness? It is amazingly simple: everybody wishes to be happy. Happiness is the goal of living beings. What's Beatus pursuit? In day-to-day life, it's quite common to hear or say, "I am incredibly happy; you are happy, what's there in; hey, be happy; no worries; I am incredibly happy for you; and so on, it goes on. "Similarly, the opposite, too, is true: "I am not happy; you are sad; the deplorables can't be happy; life is not always kind; his sad face still haunts me; and so on, it goes on." However, the million-dollar question is we, as human beings, and for that matter, all living beings, wish to pass through the process of living (life is a process) as a happy living being. People wish for it, people preach for it, people experience it, people feel it, people pursue it, and leaders promise it.

People's success is leadership's success. To know the "whys" of life has ever been the holy grail of knowledge-seeking persons. The question is: what is success? "What are one's accomplishments" a person would like to reflect upon. Is the truth of happiness of each individual unique to him or her? It's a scientific fact that it's the consciousness part, which makes a person who they are. It's the brain's repertoire, which stores the treasure of happiness or success unique to him or her. A cool-looking guy may not be happy or successful, or the converse may be true. Assuming happiness emerges from success, then what success is. According to Karl Marx, the economy is at the center stage of all relationships. Forgetting for a while the communistic interpretation of his economic structures, one fact that outstands and visible is that there is a threshold of money amount one needs to survive. There is dollar value to the resources one needs to avoid a life of misery and deplorability to break free from the shackles of poverty—

alternatively, an escape from the gravitational pull of a Deploville- a village where deplorables live.

According to Mahatma Gandhi, a person is a happy person if he or she does the same thing as he or she thinks, acts, and professes to be. In other words, what you say, what you think, and what you do are in harmony; you are happy. And this is consistent with authentic leadership. Gandhi Ji also said, "It's very simple to be happy, but it's very difficult to be simple." According to Einstein, "A calm and modest life brings more happiness than the pursuit of success combined with constant restlessness." As per the oxford dictionary, happiness is: "the state of being satisfied that something is good or right; the state of feeling or showing pleasure." George Bernard Shaw: "Happiness and beauty are by-products. Folly is the direct pursuit of happiness and beauty." According to a French poet, Guillaume Apollinaire, "Now and then it's good to pause in our pursuit of happiness and just be happy." According to George Bernard Shaw, Happiness lies in a purpose: "This is the true joy in life, being used for a purpose. He further adds, feverish, complaining, whining, selfish clod of ailments is not happiness. In brief, doing the right thing is happiness.

According to research, happiness and dollar income are correlated. However, it's flat after reaching a point on a plateau ($90,000). Economists and psychologists have taken time to collect data and find patterns of happiness related to earnings. This is what the noble laureates do. According to one research, it's 90,000 dollars, and then you break free of deplorability forces. After that, it doesn't really matter if you are a billionaire or just a millionaire. To escape deplorability gravitational pull to roam free on the "Happiness" plateau is just $90,000 earnings. According to Princeton economist Angus Deaton and famed psychologist Daniel Kahneman, happiness deteriorates if earnings are less than 60,000. With an increasing amount of earnings, happiness increases; however, after $90,000, it's all the same–no further increment into happiness. Is "diminishing rate of returns" one of the principles of economics at work? After $90,000, the return of dollar value for 'happiness' is zero.

So, what's your success story? Are you on the plateau of success/happiness? Well, it's just $90,000, or its equivalent in PPP (purchasing power parity) you need. For people to earn that much, there are two options: inherited capital or the acquired skills. For deplorables, there is the complete absence of the first option. The only path forward is skill acquisition. **Takeaway**: first, for the state actors of the day: invest in people for attaining skills as a public policy prescription. Second, for good governance, people who are endowed with capital must have confidence in the rule of law and that only good governance can provide. The rule of law directly impacts economic growth.

Is happiness, then, about hoarding big money; is it about being all-powerful; is it about knowing everything? The answer is: we don't know. It's a self-construct of a living being unique to himself or herself. However, we know that leadership plays a vital role in people's happiness and success. For existence, a dollar amount is a necessary condition. For economic growth, the rule of law is a necessary condition. The rule of law is what people expect from leadership.

A Brief Encounter with a Coyote

People do so much wrong for money only to be happy. However, happiness remains elusive. For the money, people take the risk of their existence. I had a brief encounter with a coyote who trafficked people, and people took the risk knowingly. "What do you do for a living?" I asked. "Well, I provide services for international travels and immigration," he casually answered. "I think it is a very paying business, but it has human trafficking color," I added to keep the conversation low octane. "I only charge people after their work is done and not like others who take up-front. I take care of my clients till the last destination. My way of doing it is straightforward: I take people to Singapore and then to Europe and the UK. There in the UK; they make some money and pay back the loans they owed so far. However, the destination is the USA, and still, there is one more step – I then take them to Canada. And of course, from there I arrange for the USA. My 16 persons are ready to get a USA visa – the last destination," he bragged.

A coyote's business begins when he comes in contact with an aspirant, somewhat desperate person looking for dreamland, the USA. A price is settled. It ranges from 50,000 to 70,000 US dollars till the last point. Two rates prevail ground route 50,000 and air route 70,000. In addition, the prospective asylum seeker is supposed to dole out 6000 to 10000 US dollars for the bail bond. This kind of money is arduously difficult, if not impossible, to arrange for persons of no means, the deplorables, the desperate, and the hopeless. Therefore, the argument that people in distress only seek asylum seems to be in doubt.

The possible explicable drives behind the dreamland rush seem to be improved economic benefits: the potential of better employment and superior educational facilities. Once the asylum seeker touches the dreamland, he or she is released and given a court appearance date that often is pretty long at the current prevailing situation. If the asylum seeker gets a work permit, he or she becomes a regular participant in the workforce, often needed for various businesses in the dreamland. For others, it is a work opportunity only in the shadows and significant exposure to vulnerabilities. Nevertheless, everybody starts working legally or illegally, and wages are earned. Given the minimum wages, the asylum seeker is able to send back home enough money to take care of the loan that had been taken for the payments to the coyotes. In one year or so, loans are paid back, and economically, everybody seems to be okay at the cost of the person so trafficked.

It's not a revelation that many people do perish on the long, arduous journey to dreamland. This fact is known to the risk-takers as well as to their parents and families. Yet the dreamland attraction-even fatal does not get diluted. It's incredible, the arguments some parents advance: "I have got two sons if one dies, the second is there. However, why should he die; many have not perished on the way and are doing well", they further add to suppress their guilt. This narrative tells the tale that people take the risk of their lives to find a promised land.

Success Story

One angle to look at success is an Escape from deplorability. Happiness is correlated to success, and success needs a minimum dollar value of earnings, which is necessary for life to exist. And the dollar value is $90,000. So, why do people unnecessarily chase big fairy tale dreams of being a millionaire or a billionaire to live in their fantasy world? But what is deplorability? According to Oxford Dictionary, deplorable means 'shockingly bad in quality. Deplorables do, in fact, live a life of utterly low quality.

Almost universally, cities & towns- New York, Berlin, London, New Delhi, Agra, Rio-de-Janeiro, Jakarta, et al.- have spaces for people who are unaware of where they belong to; their home address, they don't know. Ghettoes, Favela, shanties, slums, shacks, Jhopar-Patties, and so many other local names the places have, are their shelters. They live under continuous fear of showing up some psychopaths who take decisions and act to uproot them without any concern about where their following address would be, if at all. However, their search for a home address continues. Some are lucky enough to have been born with a home address; others aren't. Hillary Clinton, too, took a shot at deplorable: "You know, to just be grossly generalist, you could put half of Trump's supporters into what I call the basket of deplorables. Right? The racist, sexist, homophobic, xenophobic, Islamophobic — you name it, they are irredeemable," said she. It would seem from public figures utterances that deplorable people are the other subalterns, sub dignity people who have failed miserably in their lives and are only responsible for it. I think, right kind of policies and leadership, too, is responsible.

Democracies and Happiness

In democracies, an elaborate election process defines people's participation for a better tomorrow. During this process, promises are made by the would-be leaders more or less consistent with peoples' aspirations. People do aspire for equal society and reduced inequities, and for the rule of law. Many aspiring candidates raise voices against the wall street coyotes; they seem to promise universal health care; they seem to promise to fix the broken justice system et al. Socrates believed in democracy as a system of governance. However, according to him, to navigate a ship, the captain should be the one who should have the navigational and marine knowledge; if we choose a captain bereft of knowledge, the sinking ship is almost guaranteed. Therefore, he trusted thinking people should be the leaders.

Demagoguery is more prevalent in modern-day democracies because thinking persons do not seem to get a chance to be there. Or they seem to be reluctant to participate in the democratic processes to avoid the heat and dirt of election season. Nevertheless, people get this chance, and if they choose a sweet shop owner, who makes people sicker by distributing freebies as against the rough and tumble of an expert person, who, like a doctor, would administer a painful procedure to provide a cure for the sickness, it would be a lost opportunity for electing the right person.

Socrates stood for the right thing; however, he was punished with poison; Christ stood for the right course, was put on cross; Gandhi Ji stood for the ordinary person, was shot dead; Luther Martin King stood for the civil rights and liberties, was shot dead, too. And after their departure, we worship them all. Maybe, the collective brain of the masses is not wired to think fast enough. Or Socrates' advice for choosing a thinking person to lead has become a casualty in modern times for personal gains. Inequality in society speaks volumes. The rule of law means a good economy, and a good economy means happiness. According to Socrates, the life of a Just man is the life of happiness. For authentic leadership, it's a necessary condition to be just.

Measurement of Happiness

India's ranking on happiness (2021, World Happiness Report) stands at 139 out of 149 countries. The Delhi city's Well-Being ranking, too, is not great: at 180 out of 186 cities (Global ranking, life evaluations). Why is India so unhappy? Are we too much GDP-focused and other parameters of life evaluations are ignored? Life evaluation measures are GDP, social support, perceptions of corruption, delivery of justice, the rule of law, health, and education. If we can measure our governance and leadership on the delivery of the rule of law, it would indicate the government's performance at the time. Per life Max function, $L(x) = A * f^\alpha * s^\beta * r^\gamma$, food & shelter, and safety are the necessary conditions for life to move up the happiness ladder. This can only be possible if the rule of law prevails and the governance is sensitive to life support systems, including education and health. Happiness, though, is subjective, and parameters like neighbor's income play a role in a person's happiness. However, measures like the basic level of income that takes economic worries off a person's mind are measurable. The rule of law and corruption indicators, too, are measurable. For instance, in the following Figure 7.3, it is clear that economic anxieties are critical to people's happiness.

Figure 7.3 (Life Evaluations)

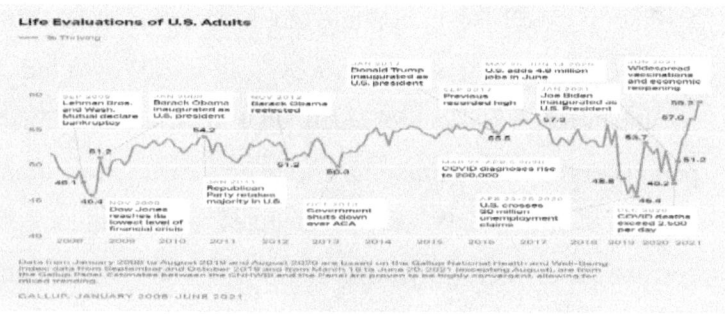

During recessions 2009 and 2020, induced by the financial meltdown and covid 19, the people's happiness plummeted. People were more worried. Partially it is explainable by the uncertain environment – uncertainty increases entropy into the ecosystem of governance (increase in entropy, increases disorder and randomness). As a consequence, financial anxieties shot up and affected lives.

At the same time, it is also clear that to be happy requires more than income (Figure 7.4).

Figure 7.4 (GDP & Happiness)

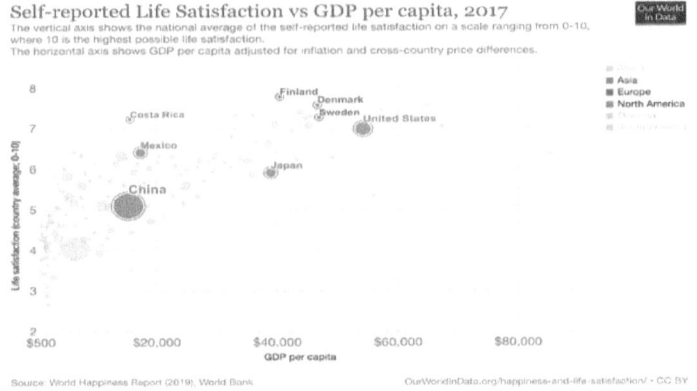

Figure 7.4, how to explain Costa Ricans' or Mexicans' happiness more than Japan's. For sure, GDP does not explain it all. As Paul Krugman, Noble Laureate, explains it, "health and relationships play a leading role in happiness." According to him, "Americans differ vastly from one another in how happy they are with their lives, but most of that variation reflects personal factors rather than money: There are miserable billionaires and cheerful families barely scraping by." "Happiness resides not in possessions, and not in gold, happiness dwells in the soul." – Democritus.

****

8

Toxic leadership

Working environments in many organizations and at the political level in many countries aren't what employees and people aspire for. Many employees at Goldman Sachs, an organization people would love to get a job, have complained of a suffocating working environment. Even Amazon, the darling of many, seems to have a work-horse culture to squeeze the last drop of sweat out of the people who work there. Leadership is about ideas and doing the right things. In Goldman Sachs, according to some of its employees, the culture quotient has gone down to zero under the current leadership at the top level. The secret sauce – a culture of this organization, the moral fiber, has been shredded to pieces. Compromising clients' best interest and morally corrupt in increasing profits of the organization would ultimately move away from clients and harming itself. Employees making more money only are likely to be promoted to positions of influence. The right type of culture that used to be once, working for the right reasons in the clients' best interest, seems to have vanished, and some employees with a spine have put forward their resignations. Leadership at Goldman Sachs forced employees to work 90 hours a week in a suffocating environment full of fear of losing if not complying with the wishes of the top seating creatures.

So is the case in many countries: for instance, in Myanmar, democratic forces have been made zero; in India, police would register cases of treason against peaceful protesters for their civil rights; in the USA, too, the country that considers itself as the beacon of democracy, some states (Republican governed) are rushing through legislative bills that would undermine voting rights for some communities. An elected person congresspeople gets arrested just for a knock on the door is beyond comprehension. Toxicity of leadership is manifested in fear of the people doing and standing for the right things. In the long run, though, such organizations end up in bankruptcy, and countries like Turkey face financial disaster putting their people in misery. Doctors and scientists working at the White House under the Trump administration opened up after his departure about how toxic it was to work under his leadership.

Consequences: Trump lost his job; people lost their loved ones; and economic costs went up high.

Leaders and business executives holding a position of power have the power to create an environment consistent with people giving their best for the accomplishment of their assigned tasks, or they can create an environment where everybody feels stifled and unhappy. Toxicity they bring to the workplace or to the people they lead has all the potential of dangerous outcomes in demolishing democratic institutions. Even the very survival of democracy is arm twisted and pushed in a death spiral. Recent happenings (Jan 6, 2021) at DC Washington, the capitol of the wealthiest country in the world, witnessed turbulence created under the watch of the head of the state. Toxic leaders have the potential of burning stuff at the cost of millions of people. But what is toxic leadership?

History is full of unconcerned and destructive leaders from Henry King VIII to Jeff Skilling, and to name a few, Idi Amin, Uganda (Approx.1925-2003), Nicolae Ceausescu, Romania (1918-1989), Augusto Pinochet, Chile (1915-2006), Kim Il-sung, North Korea (1912-1994), Francois "Papa Doc" Duvalier, Haiti (1907-1971), Mao

Zedong, China (1893-1976), Francisco Franco, Spain (1892-1975), Adolf Hitler, Germany (1889-1945), Joseph Stalin, Russia (1878-1953), Benito Mussolini, Italy (1883-1945). Dictators care for only one person: "Self." Whatever comes in their way, it is removed with brutal force. Fear is the tool they use. Well, this kind of stuff doesn't even fall in the category of leadership. It's just toxic. These types of persons have a manipulative way of exploiting people's fears and uncertainties. People get captivated by the illusions they provide for and get trapped.

Traits they display include lying to followers to bolster a great vision, holding to power by undermining democratic institutions, actions that marginalize and intimidate others, enormous ego and arrogance, incompetency, narcissism, fear and greed, instability and fragility, manipulative, least concern for the people, self-gain, subversion of ethical and democratic institutions, stifle criticism, and violate human rights. In the Bible of Army of the USA, the following appears for defining a toxic leader, "This leader lacks concern for others and the climate of the organization, which leads to short- and long-term negative effects. The toxic leader operates with an inflated sense of self-worth and acute self-interest. Toxic leaders consistently use dysfunctional behaviors to deceive, intimidate, coerce, or unfairly punish others to get what they want for themselves. The negative leader completes short-term requirements by operating at the bottom of the continuum of commitment, where followers respond to the positional power of their leader to fulfill requests. This may achieve results in the short term but ignores the other leader competency categories of leads and developments. Prolonged use of negative leadership to influence followers undermines the followers' will, initiative, and potential and destroys unit morale."

Whenever a violent or suicide case is investigated, the focus goes in the direction of the perpetrator's mental health. In Iraq, a general noticed that there was an abnormal increase in suicide cases, and he employed a professor to investigate the mental health issues with the soldiers. Professor Matsuda was assigned this task. The professor turned the needle of investigation on the role of toxic leadership. According to his finding, soldiers did have personal problems; however, it had something to do with the leaders who pushed them to an edge and made them take their own lives. This led to the conclusion that toxic leaders need to be identified and coached on to improve upon. In one of the states in India, a senior police officer used to make the life of a junior hell by calling him at the wrong hours of the night for problems not existing. Another officer faced the same issues and devised his own method to deal with them. He would solve some trivial matters in the dead of night and call him, out of design, at the wrong inconvenient hours of the night. He turned the tables back on him and took the toxicity out of him. The fact, however, remains that toxic seniors-leaders do exist and seldom are identified. Outcomes are difficult and painful for juniors. The question is how to identify them and coach or train them to come out of their toxicity to be effective and to become authentic leaders.

According to one study, in India, 34% of bureaucrats suffer from the ailment of narcissism-toxic leadership. Toxic leaders are more concerned about their own promotion and would go to any extent to self-elevate and inflate self-worth. They hardly give credit to their team members and try to steal all the credit for themselves. An authentic leader would always give credit to team members, and rightly so. Without a team giving its best, tasks cannot be accomplished efficiently. It's bizarre that some bureaucrats like making people wait outside doors to make themselves feel important. I joined my first posting and wished to call upon a senior. I waited for 45 minutes to find out only that the gentleman was playing with his stuff inside. I wonder till this day why the heck was I given an appointment only. Later, I found out it is a customary practice among this class of people to feel great. How irrational! Another friend shared his experience about his boss (senior IAS officer reporting to a very senior IAS officer), which is like this: the meeting would start after the office hours, and before the meeting really begins, the juniors would wait for hours (in the waiting room- so-called) and then some crap stuff would happen in the meeting (meetings hardly solve problems in bureaucracy). The meeting would be formally declared as concluded by the dark. His pain didn't end with the meeting ending. He didn't have a vehicle to go back home, and no other alternative transport was available. Junior officer expected to be dropped off along with the senior in a pool car. However, the senior refused to give him a lift, instead asked him to wait till the driver comes back after dropping him off. It was not one freaky incidence; it was the characteristic typical behavior of the senior officer to feel self-high.

However, inside, the person was very fragile: he would just choke in front of politicians. I could realize the guy had some serious psychological issues. Such cool-looking guys, when they hold positions of power, are, in fact, capable of driving juniors to a cliff. And in one case, as the rumors have it, an officer did take his life. Such is the toxicity that some narcissist leaders take pleasure in, which is dangerous and fraught with risky outcomes. In the world of psychiatry, it's a defense mechanism they use to hide in to keep their fragility buried deep down.

Recent happenings in response to the pandemic have brought toxic leaders to the fore. COVID-19 took the world by surprise, and in a time of uncertainty, authoritarian tendencies crept in; lockdowns were declared, and everything came to a standstill. There emerged a role of health officials. The USA has the highest infection and mortality rate despite the highest per capita cost on health. People voted the President out of office. The top epidemiologist spoke, "I feel liberated." Yet another principal health officer said, "her office never gave the graphs and data that the White House presented." Until he got out of the office, none of these officers dared to speak facts because of fear – threats were given to the officers and their families. Such is the outcome of toxic leadership. Narcissist leaders never have a concern for people. What only matters to them are their interests? However, the question is: how these toxic leaders reach a position of power and bring home hell?

Farmers' protest in India (Jan 2021, New Delhi) is a case in point about toxic leadership at the political level. In a democratic setup, the voice of people matters. When people have no trust in the state actors, and the state favors authoritarian measures, the outcome is no good. Historically, a conflict exists between the two parties – Elite and the Citizens (Wall Street VS Main Street). The fact of the matter is that a small elite is well organized, and most of the population – a majority (for that matter in any country. For instance, in the UK, only 15% of people effectively participate in the political process. And it is not much different in many other developed nations, much less in non-developed countries) is unorganized. De Jure democratic systems get hijacked by de facto political systems (many democracies are authoritative de facto – parliamentary processes get hijacked by a small group). For instance, in India, if someone writes a critique against the state actors, they become the subject of torture despite more than 70 years of the republic. The persistence of economic disadvantage persists against the majority despite a change in the political de jure democratic changes. I remember it very well during a 'Meet the local CM' at Ahmedabad IIM course of IAS officers; the then CM said, "Britishers have left the country, and they left behind the civil service framework. The framework served British interests as against the peoples' interests then; now the current political bosses have found it convenient to use the same framework to their advantage." It's empirically observed in many other countries, despite a de jure change in political systems, economic institutions persist. In other words, de facto power distribution still exists with a few organized and the majority, unorganized, continue in not much better economic fate.

In the USA (south), slavery was abolished long ago; however, the plantation still exists, and the labor wages have not gone up competitively. Here in the current farmers' agitation, farmers in India, the affected party was the last to be consulted before the parliamentary process of passing the laws. A small group of elites took the decision, and now their ego has attained more importance than the laws themselves. The bigger question remains: how long the divide of elite VS everyday citizens will persist? How long would the ordinary person not get well-deserved competitive wages, and how long would the elite continue to pull economic rents? In the present case, how long the majority – the farmers, would be able to hold as against the organized minority of political and bureaucratic elites? Despite de jure changes, farmers are still disadvantaged, and remunerative prices to their crops are a distant dream. By putting them in a contract regime of corporation's modern era of economic concentration in a few corporations, (who de facto pull strings in policy formulation: it's common knowledge that the de facto powers purchase policy decisions), farmers position is not going to change. Exploitation would continue.

According to Oxfam report (2020), during the pandemic, the wealth of the top few in India increased so much that it would be sufficient to keep rural jobs in India for ten years. One hundred twenty-two million people lost jobs, and 75% belonged to the informal sector. "The mass exodus on foot triggered by the sudden lockdown and the inhuman beatings, disinfection and quarantine conditions, the informal workers were subjected to, turned a health emergency into a humanitarian crisis." More than 300 people died while the migrant workers were left to their fate for starvation, suicides, road and rail accidents, police brutality, and denial of any medical help. National Human commission recorded more than 2500 human rights violations. If this is not toxic leadership, then what is? Recently, a health minister in the state of Punjab has been reported to have diverted a large number of vaccines for selling at a much higher price in the market. What more toxic leadership could prevail? In many states of India, past, and present, heads of the states seem to be anthemic to protesters and democratically organized criticism, which is the hallmark of present-day democracies. They use intimidating, brutal police force to arrest innocent people. They are demagogues; they are not leaders.

Long back, as trainee officers, we (a group of officers) had to visit a rural setting, a village in the state of UP. We heard fables of dacoits. Special police protection was organized to maintain safety. Again, after many years I was assigned a job of an election observer in the same state of UP. I took this opportunity to visit a remote village. Subconsciously I was interested in looking for a change in the village living conditions after so many years. I interacted with the local people. They were welcoming and polite as ever. To my surprise, people still talked about dacoits and the village elite. The fact of the matter is that the battle between organized minorities and the unorganized majority hasn't gone away. In this battle of un-equals, the strong wins. People live under constant fear of reprisal. Lately, I had a chance to visit my village school, yet again to find out if there is a change since I graduated. There, too, instead of upgradation, things have gone downhill. "Who is interested in the education of minority small farmers' (and others in the village) kids," I thought. It's a distant dream. Old tribalism somehow persists despite de jure political changes. Isn't it toxic leadership that cares little for people's concerns?

The fact is that toxic leaders do get into positions, and they exist. How to get rid of them, kill their toxicity, or bring them home to become normal leaders is the question. One of the reasons toxic leaders continue in their positions is top-down evaluation. From an evolutionary perspective, self-aggrandizing behavior is expected. However, in a civilized world, conditions are needed to keep the toxicity away. In animal societies, toxic leaders prevail. In many cases, dominant individuals don't behave likewise with people who seem to care for subordinates and the people they lead. Toxic leaders intimidate subordinates and extract as much as possible.

Authentic Leadership

Authentic leadership is devoid of falsehoods and lies. Authentic leaders are there for the people and not for themselves. They don't take pleasure in the misery of others by shedding crocodile tears. When a situation, as uncertain as to the pandemic, arises and control seems to vanish in the thin air, human instinct and management training may lead leaders/decision-makers in unchartered territory, and mistakes are likely to happen. For instance, installing disinfectant channels in India was a good-faith mistake out of panic. However, a test of steel lies in fire: leadership's crucible test is crisis management. The right type of information only helps. Things happened without even consulting the epidemiologist/scientists. It does require collecting the correct type of information from the best available sources for effective and good faith management of things. It's information only that reduces entropy in the system during a crisis. Pressing a panic button certainly is not consistent with good leadership. Decisive decisions are required in moments of uncertainty. Urgent, honest, good faith, interactive, and recognizing mistakes and immediate corrective steps help in such situations. In simple and plain words, good leadership is about people and not about the leaders themselves. If self takes precedence over management of things, it's a good signal for inauthentic leadership.

Governor of New York, Andrew Cuomo, Harvey Weinstein, Carly Fiorina, and many others who chose intimidators' leadership style over leadership with humility and good faith fell from grace finally. According to The Wall Street Journal, "tough guys will finish last." The Reign of such leaders ends up in disaster only. In India, state actors suddenly declared lockdown, thereby bringing misery to the migrant workers who lost jobs and were left to their fate on roads. However, leadership in New Zealand took courage, communicated with people, and made things clear what New Zealand was up to, even though the number of cases was just 59 or so. The head of the state proved and displayed the kind of leadership people aspire for. She acted urgently and transparently and put people first. It benefited both: the leader as well the people she led.

Contrary to this, in India, people suffered, and leadership did lose the people's trust. In a way, both proved to be losers: the state actors and the people who suffered the authoritarian commands for unscientific solutions- a spray of chemicals on the migrant laborers. Authentic leadership is a win-win game.

For a leader, there would be occasions for decision making when forces are opposite, and a situation emerges like a dilemma. What do you do? Simple: go the right direction. It's credibility and trust that are critical in a leadership story. The bigger question, however, is: how to win credibility and trust? In uncertain times, leaders have none. A large number of write-ups, some evidenced, some opinionated, exist in the literature on this topic. Some theories support intimidators: there is research that supports democratic styles. The fact of the matter is that everybody is interested in what works: failure has no template. Toxic leadership may have a day of success, but in the long run, they kiss the dust.

It's not uncommon to wade through rainy days; we do have "Cross-Road-Moments,"; and there are occasions when "approach-avoidance" conflicts catch up with life.

Targeted objects/subjects seem to have pull and repulsive powers simultaneously. People do get caught up between two fires; people do face dilemmas; people do find themselves in cognitive dissonance; people face Hobson's choice; people do find themselves in catch 22 situations. It's a war zone; it's a battle of raw instincts vs. acquired intelligence. The question is: how to get out of it; how to resolve a conflict? Should you let your home/workplace into a war zone over issues of significant collateral damages as consequences of intended or unintended actions? Actions do have consequences, for sure. The answer is simple: know it first, then make a U-turn, or change yourself; do not justify wrong actions; if you do, you sure are in a psychoville.

A leader's mindfulness of a situation is helpful. For instance, Vice President Michael Pence and other leaders of the congress and Senate found themselves in a life-threatening situation while performing (Jan 6, 2021) their constitutional duty. Indeed, great leadership prevailed. It was an enormous show of courage, vision, and mindfulness of doing the right thing. Democracy was almost put in a death spiral by none other than the head of the state. In democracies, leadership at the institutional level is critical for its survival. If one who assaults free and fair democratic institutions, not a toxic leader, then who? According to the authors (Bob Woodward) of the book 'Peril,' democratic institutions were clearly diminished by the state actors at the time.

****

9

Neuroscience and Leadership

Leadership is all about people and people have brains. A leader is also a human being and has a brain. Understanding as what brain contains within helps. At the base level knowledge, the science of brain and central nervous system is neuroscience. But what neuroscience has got to do with leadership? The answer is: a lots. Insights into neuroscience tell us that every time we interact with people and other external environment, our neural pathways are affected: old may get reinforced, or new may get formed. Whatever we know today about brain is possible because of advanced research in the field of neuroscience, which is a multidisciplinary approach including, clinical psychology, molecular biology, computer science and mathematical modeling. If leaders are aware of scientific knowledge of brain, it equips them with information for efficient decision making and solving problems.

For instance, the knowledge that every time a person passes through an episode of fear, or trauma, he or she damages his or her DNA, double-strand breaks (DSB). Simply put, brain cells are damaged and repair process takes its toll. It results in dangerous outcomes (neurodegeneration and cognitive decline) for the person who is passing through it. Toxic leaders are responsible for this invisible damage to the people they lead unconsciously. On the contrary, a leader well equipped with this information would solve problems not through shock and awe, but by being straight with the people. Research at MIT has shown that "Impaired DNA repair of these recurrent DNA breaks which are generated as part of brain activity could result in genomic instability that contribute to aging and disease in the brain." Isn't it an amazing neurological insight for a leader to lead people with empathy? Demagogues aren't authentic leaders and neuroscience validates it. People got to be watchful in electing such persons to the high office. It would end up in self-harm only.

In the constitution of India, there exists a provision for the scientific temper. (directive Principles, 51A. It shall be the duty of every citizen of India; (h) to develop the scientific temper, humanism, and the spirit of inquiry and reform). The scientific thought process helps to solve problems. It's a promising idea that natural laws, tried and tested, have applications for social sciences and social ecosystems. Natural laws like entropy (disorder, reactance), physics of dominoes effect (amplification of forces) have lots to offer for understanding, knowing, and solving problems of social ecosystems like governance.

Research in neuroscience and cognitive science unleashes new knowledge to gain insights and improve upon personal and leadership behavior. Leaders' primary task is decision-making, problem-solving, and leading the folks with empathy and humility. It is important how they communicate and connect with people, whether in the political world or the business. How people behave, why they do what they do, has been a subject matter of research. Psychoanalysts, psychiatrists, and now neuroscientists have thrown their hat in the ring of the truth-finding mission. Both psychoanalysts and psychiatrists emphasize the unconscious that plays a significant role in human behavior. As for the neuroscientists, with the arrival of fMRI machines, emphasis has shifted to the physical part of the brain. So far, what we know, a normal human brain is stuffed with 80 to 100 billion neurons and thousands of dendrites attached with each neuron that forms the neurological pathways for transporting signals from sensory organs to activated organs for accomplishing tasks.

There is other stuff in the brain like glial cells (so far, research has not found much about how they play a role in the entire process of communication). A lot of research has been done on the brain slices of the Noble laureate Einstein. So far, there is no indication that he had more neurons in his brain than a normal brain. However, some scientists have suggested his neurons were more thickly populated than an average person's brain. One of the scientists has gone even to the extent (by studying the photos of his brain) that he did have an extra sulcus fold, cautiously adding, though, it might lead to phrenology (reading too much from the bumps on the cranium), which is not much scientifically supported.

As more scientific knowledge emerges from neuroscientists' experiments and research, more insights become handy to study its relevance to leadership styles and leaders' behavior. The idea is: how neurology plays a role behind decisions making of leaders leading the world of politics and business? For instance, decision-making involves steps beginning from sensing information and knowing options to finally taking a decision after evaluating each option and choosing the best. Actions have consequences. If outcomes of decisions were consistent with goals in the past, similar decisions for similar circumstances are likely to be repeated. Neuroscientists study through fMRI machines what goes into the brain while making such decisions. It has been revealed that fast decision-making is to be taken immediately in emergent situations; and in such situations actions precede decisions. Isn't it an amazing finding? It simply means that the brain has automatically collected information signals, evaluated options, chosen the optimal, and executed it before the conscious decision even has been activated. It's like a brain on autopilot.

Why is this important for the people to be aware of, especially those who make decisions that impact millions of people? In the world of hubris-laden heads of the states and business leaders, it sounds like a warning signal for a complex and dynamic situation. A leader is a human being who is an outcome of his or her position, learnings, experiences, and unique skills. Awareness of this uniqueness is what the neuroscientists emphasize. For instance, leaders are appreciated who advocate decisions by gut feeling. People admire them for their cojones. The admiration and success in a situation get embedded into the subconscious of the brain. This would work like an algo or hard wiring in a brain's physiological dispositions. Whenever an analogous situation would emerge, the brain would be on autopilot, and a decision would have been implemented before a conscious decision had been taken.

Realizing brains' limitation, leaders would like to surround themselves with people of expertise and listen to other alternatives. This would have the benefit of having additional algos written in other persons' brains by way of their unique learnings and experiences. This would result in a much more extensive knowledge tool pool to extract from and solving problems efficiently. This neurological knowledge adds only to the fact that the unconscious does play a significant role. The conscious must recognize that the unconscious needs to be dug out by carefully listening to experts. They don't have enough to offer. Nevertheless, it helps in being on the right course.

Neurological insights help in identifying barriers and arranging for training. Neurological pathways are created after each exposure to information, experience, education, and training, and it becomes critical to a success story to have the right kind of exposure. For the state actors, it guides us to focus on useful information exposures. For instance, what we expose people to, gets written into their brains in the shape of algos that would sub-consciously guide their future actions. Put in other words, the quality of education, the quality of training, and the quality of experience matters. If rogue algos get written into the brain because of traumatic experiences, they keep interfering with the right course decisions.

Neurodiversity

End of the day, it's people who matter. In an organization for the personnel department to hire people, neurodiversity makes sense. People with diverse information exposures and unique experiences bring home a diverse skillset of knowledge that becomes a pool of knowledge available to an organization. Another way of looking at it is that people with skill gaps may be professionally trained and equipped with the skillset consistent with job requirements. Neurological insights make the training part extremely important. Most of the time, training time is taken as a sabbatical or a relaxed outing. However, neuroscientists would recommend that training needs seriousness it is supposed to. Our brains are wired to learn by observation, from trial-and-error experimentation, and all these learnings get hard-wired into it. Over time, it becomes a part of the algos pool written in our brain. Knowledge of how a brain is structured and how it functions can be of immense help in developing frameworks for embedding desirable algos.

Limitations of Brain

Our brain has limits, though. Neuroscientists have indicated that the brain gets confused if choices are limitless and no decision output pops out. Brains do have physiological constraints. Context matters and the brain again gets confused. For instance, a circle surrounded by bigger circles looks small, and the same circle surrounded by smaller circles looks bigger than it looks in the first setting. There are optical illusions that the brain cannot handle cleanly and squarely. The question is, how does it matter? The answer lies in being aware of these limitations of the brain and wrapping an arm around them for efficient decision-making and problem-solving. If a leader with hubris ignores more efficient alternatives, they are likely to make dangerous mistakes. It only tells us that hubris has no scientific backing. The more we know what's there inside, the more we can deal with situations that otherwise look overwhelming. For instance, framing effect matters to be aware of as how options are set in addition to the options themselves. Thus, setting or context matters for decision making. A wartime hero may fail in a peacetime situation. However, if one knows that the brain has physiological limits and is tuned to listen to the counsel of wiser people, problems can be better dealt with. The understanding, brain as a physiological organism, indeed, helps. It's like knowing the hardware and software part of a computer to make use of it. Of course, reducing humans to this analogy is fraught with problems. Nevertheless, it offers a perspective to look at our brains.

William James wrote in his book The Principles of Psychology 1890 that by early age 25, we had fixed our neural pathways, and it's like a personality and character of an individual etched in stone. It is supported by the latest research, too. However, there is good news: change in neural pathways is possible, and stuck neural pathways could be broken. In addition, regeneration of neurons is possible. The key idea is that there is a lot of flexibility and plasticity (the ability of the brain to rewrite neural pathways). Therefore, exposure to correct information is extremely important. Neural pathways do get written at any age. Research shows that neurogeneration is possible and embedded pathways could be broken, and new wiring is possible. But it requires conscious steps and focused attention. According to Professor Swart, "conscious processing of inputs, conscious decision making, complex problem solving, memorizing complex concepts, planning, strategizing, self-reflection, regulating our emotions and channeling energy from them, exercising self-control and willpower" helps. Other steps that enhance rewiring include continuous practice and a setting where the environment is consistent with the desired goal of rewriting.

Do we have a reset button in our brain?

As the saying goes, we learn from the past, act in the present, and plan for the future. But the question is: can we unlearn the learned and undo the past? Can we behave differently in the present, given the past? Or history repeats itself? Learning is a process that begins with parents and family – observation is a great tool that works consciously and unconsciously to write routines and subroutines in the brain, given nature's hard codes. End of the day, it's an input-output game, and a brain is a biological machine. However, unlike computers, input in the brain gets stuck inside memory – the hippocampus, and 'delete' isn't a click away. Many of the subroutines, written over through observation, learning, training, and experience, get kicked in automatically from the unconscious as and when a stimulus shows up. It's like being on autopilot. Human beings act and repeat acts, and learning attains its shape, and it defines the persona of an individual. Temperament, character, integrity, et al. traits start to define a person as an individual grows along the growth and development trajectory. Here is the thing: can we unlearn the rogue learned behavior?

The priori is the very existence of human beings as biological machines. This machine is unique and functions in unique ways. Let us agree that the starting point is genetic code: the code the biological machine comes with – two gametes and one zygote. Analogously, say, computer hardware with its primary information processing capacities. Rest has got to be written and rewritten in the shape of subroutines and routines, the functional codes to make the machine – the life, as a functional biological power machine. Well, the idea of treating human beings as machines may not be likable to many. However, the fact remains that we are biological unique machines and function autonomously most of the time. Yes, Brain is on autopilot, most of the time. Freewill seems to be a luxury of few and that, too, not in abundance. According to research in neuroscience, one fact that has emerged is that we know little about our brain: there are still lots of unknowns in the space between our two ears. It has amply been demonstrated in fMRI labs that humans' actions precede decision making. What little we know is that it is two% of the weight of our body and consumes twenty percent of energy; neuron cells and glial cells hold the secret of its functioning. Limited knowable has been possible by using fMRI machines and the computing power of the computers we have today. However, to process all the information that goes through interacting 100 billion neurons and dendrites with thousands of nodes for connections within an average brain is far beyond the existing computing technology. The net conclusion is whatever we know is through our unique experiences and learnings, which may be true or false, like lobotomy experiments conducted by one of the most botched noble prize winners.

The question is: how to rewrite the codes in the brain to reset it? Is resetting possible? If yes, what are the methods available to people? Rewriting codes would be difficult because the 'delete' option is not available: memories in human beings do not get washed away. Many of the memories remain as fresh as ever. These writings on the proteins in the brain are a source of information that gets kicked in autonomously, and the unconscious plays a significant role in immediate responses. With these scientific facts, which we know today, unlearning would be an intense exercise to give place to targeted learning. Training of killer whales, if not impossible, would be an arduous and time and capital-intensive proposition. People do change, but fewer than desired. Even if they wish, they cannot as developmental stage codes aren't easy to erase and rewriting becomes all the more challenging. It's like the new code would have to delete the old one and take the command from the newer one. In other words, 'old habits die hard' prevails. However, with determined efforts unlearning is possible, and lots of space is there to rewrite. A precondition, however, is knowing first what to be deleted and what to be rewritten. Self-redemption is possible: it doesn't need a miracle; all it needs a need to change and determination and persistence. There is no reset button in the brain: however, with an investment in time and consciousness, the unconscious can be defeated. As a state policy or for parents, the best path forward is "catch them young" – write the right codes at the right time to avoid the inflated costs of deletion later. Miracles do happen, and self-redemption is possible. Learned helplessness can be triumphed. Never say, "Shouganai."

A leader's brain need to be aware of the unconscious processes and then need to be resetting the neural pathways consistent with the requirements of leading. Leadership is about the people; it's about the customers and employees; in a family situation, it's about the family members; it's about the pupils in a teaching or training setting. This awareness leads to authentic leadership. Neuroscience knowledge helps a political leader, an army general, a business executive, a parent, or a teacher to rewrite the neural pathways if not already there in the brain. The brain is the repertoire of the tools available to a leader to lead. Most of the time, the brain is on autopilot and takes decisions and executes tasks after evaluating all the tools available within the brain's store – the neural pathways. Without any doubt, neuroscience holds promise for outstanding leadership in all situations -complex and dynamic.

Not Too Late

As for learning and resetting neural pathways, it is never late. Is it too late to graduate at 84? Yes, eighty-four years of age. It was a wonderful day at TD Garden Boston. Usually, people go there for Celtics NBA games. On 26th May 2017, it was a different gathering, though. University of Massachusetts Boston commencement ceremony bounced up with unmatched excitement and cheers: "you have done it– that's my baby"; "that's my kid"; "there she is: Jennifer!!" "Jimmy, she is on the big TV screen! Up there!" Indeed, it was a graduates' day. Students from 49 states of the USA and 100 countries worldwide presented themselves in diverse dresses, culturally different, vibrant, and exuberant to receive their diplomas. But there was something in the air; there was something common; there was only one thing that represented all the countries, all the states, and all the cultures; there was one common thread that wove them all in one category: yes, you guessed it right;

before anything else, they were all students, and they were all graduates by now. We were looking only for one face in the big crowd, someone we only recognized, someone who made her family and parents proud, Jennifer Lynn Malik. So did others look for someone they knew and loved and cared for. Yes, happiness's ultimate source seemed to be hidden somewhere in the family only.

The Chancellor Motely outstood in the gathering – a leader who led this public university to great heights. Usually, privately managed educational universities are looked upon with lots of preferences. In the USA, the public education system and private education institutes compete. It is no hidden secret that in the world's top private institute, "Harvard University," there are professors of eminence who graduated from public high schools only. Whenever a student passed through the handshake machine to come out a graduate, there were lots of cheers and applause. However, this time, this was different. It was a standing ovation and lasted longer. Motley, too, walked down the podium to provide a hug to an extraordinary graduate of the day: a graduate who did honor to all the women, completing her graduation at 84. Yes, this great-grandma offers an illustration. It's never too late to learn and live with honor. Neuroscience validates it.

****

10

Black Swan Events and Leadership

Historically, the phrase got into the mainstream in medieval Europe in philosophical discourses and on publishing the book by Nassim Nicholas Taleb, The Black Swan: The Impact of the Highly Improbable. In theory, black swan events are rare to happen and predictable in the past only. Such events have enormous consequences and couldn't have been predicted. In the statistical normal distribution, black swan events are the happenstances of tail-end events. These events happen out of nowhere, and "expect-the-unexpected" wins. Black swan events are inexplicably happenings beyond the statistical and probabilistic models drawn from empirical observations over several years. Patterns seem to kiss dust, and forecasting models collapse, and monstrous things happen. Whatever the way it is understood, it is an unknown-unknown situation. The fact of life, however, is that they do happen and catch you by surprise. In the management world, risk management is a key consideration. How to meet the risk situations, then, is a challenge to the leadership of the moment.

(Black Swan Image Source: Google.com)

"The test of steel lies in fire," as one saying goes. A crisis is a time when leaders meet with destiny - crucible test, the grit they have to show, the leadership claims they have got to prove, the unchartered waters they have got to navigate. It's a time of success or failure; it's a time of do or die, no middle paths. What is a crisis, though? Crises are the tail events in the normal distribution of happenings. Put another way, extreme unexpected events happen, and everybody is taken by surprise, scrambling for immediate survival solutions. It's a plague with no known medicine; it's a fire to be fought without firefighters; it's a flood to be navigated without a boat; it's a drought to be survived without water in sight; it's a battle to be fought with little resources. Black swan events show in various forms: World Wars, pandemics, plagues, fall of Soviet Union, 2007-2008 fiscal crisis, Covid 19, are examples of black swan events. Such events shatter all illusion of control and certainty. Uncertain people meet with unknowns with unknown solutions. Leaders scramble for solutions to keep order and drill in some confidence among people.

Recently (2021), the state of Texas in the USA faced severe cold with an extreme event of snow and low temperatures. Everything came to a halt: low temperatures froze the water, and power plants got dysfunctional. People were without electricity and water, and many perished within their cold and freezing houses midst plenty. Indeed, a crisis situation – a black swan event. Senator Ted Cruz escaped to Mexico to have a break; Governor Abbot blamed green projects (solar and wind energy projects) for the grid failure. The blame game is not uncommon in failing situations. However, it's the leadership that does not have this luxury – leaders got to calm down the situation, address peoples' concerns, and be with them. Ted Cruz wasn't there; so was the Governor, looking for blames instead of solving problems. The first and foremost requirement of leadership in a black swan event is a leader physically be there. It establishes trust among the people in the leadership that would solve problems; there is uncertainty about nothing happening. Put another way: it helps calm midst misery.

Thinking of a swan, however, a bird's picture swirls into mind. In the real world, though, black swan events mean how to deal with risk. Things go as bad as they would; people react as irrationally as they would; order makes way to disorder, and people in the driving seat scramble for solutions as fast they could to bring back some semblance of sanity out of insane happenings. Uncertainty is the fact of life, and we live in an uncertain world. For instance, events like the 9/11 COVID-19 pandemic take people by surprise and render life paralyzed. In March 2011, the Fukushima disaster – earthquake and tsunami, is another event that took the life out of gear. Reactor meltdown brought along misery. Criticism raises its ugly head: "had we planned, it could have been avoided." However, unexpected stuff happens, and leaders got to deal with it. Intuition and experience at the job come in handy in solving complex, risky problems. Research suggests, with data and science-based management, risk can be mitigated.

Leadership, without any doubt, is about managing crisis-driven events, among other things. For instance, climate change events have given rise to a question: are we prepared for the environment black swan events? In Paris, COP 21 (Conference of Parties, 21st meeting under the domain of UNFCCC), for the first time, a large body of heads of the states gathered to express a concern for the degrading climate. It appeared that a political will had emerged as a common global interest for human existence. However, later President Trump dissociated from it. Aren't the extreme weather events (which took place in Uttarakhand, J&K, India) enough reason to plan for such extreme and catastrophic events?

There are situations when leadership functions in diverse ways. One is transactional leadership: set goals, meet customers, achieve goals, communicate effectively. Second is strategic leadership: this kind of leadership ventures into stuff not done earlier. It involves vision and new direction. In India, for instance, the district level position involves both: transactional – routine work and strategic and crisis management leadership – a sudden eruption of law-and-order problems, natural disasters, innovative initiatives that define and solve a problem.

Strategic level leadership requires hard conscious decision-making and problem-solving. Time becomes of the essence. For instance, what do we do for a sudden big-time accident in an area or a big fire in a jurisdictional area? The immediate focus would be on saving lives-rescue measures and securing a law and order situation. Unexpected, uncertain events do happen, and if one is not prepared for such events, it would be a complex and challenging proposition. For instance, heavy rains deluge a whole city, roads get blocked, and people are on their rooftops shouting for help. Would it be enough just to hear those shouts and not to be of any help? Of course, not. Strategic leadership requires to have visioned the unexpected and be ready for such unexpected events.

COVID-19 is an extreme black swan event that shook the entire world. Leaders scrambled for solutions, experimented, and doubled down to keep sanity and order. Employees were sent home, and people worked from anywhere but the office, retrofitting essential workplaces to carry on. Different leadership styles got into action. Leaders were empathy-driven for mitigating people's pain; however, working non-stop hours and pushing to limits was the order of the day. Crisis management simply means you survive or die. Everything so transparent, universe watching, leadership needed to hard charge and move forward. Front line workers were hard-pressed to function even under risky settings. Many managed to lead from the front, and many kept back and got the flak. Yes, "Be There" indeed worked effectively. The crisis involves innovative ideas and resilience. Crisis brings people together and people understand problems from a close encounter with existence. For instance, everything seemed out of control and uncertain during the pandemic and many CEOs kept away from their families just to keep them safe from the virus. People faced inequalities that became so transparent – long food queues. The value of front-line workers got all the attention it would ever have had gotten. Many doctors and nurses perished, and many were forced to stay away from homes and work under adverse settings.

Why do humans underestimate unexpected events? The answer is simple: Humans are humans, and they have limitations. Human behavior is irrational often. Humans have what they have as a consequence of biological dividends and learnings. Learning is a consequence of observation, education, and unique human experience as one grows and adapts. It's a kind of complex and dynamic affair. During this complete process of survival, irrationality becomes an integral part of the persona humans carry. Cognitive bias is not uncommon; so is confirmation bias. In the age of modern science, human behavior is a consequence of inputs in a processing machine we call it brain. The "Garbage in Garbage out" principle holds good. In a world of management overloaded with quantitative techniques, patterns, and probabilistic models, figures only matter. Pattern after pattern tend to confirm leadership bias; they fail to see the red signals blipping alongside. Leaders become so overindulged they don't even want to see the obvious except the statistics on the paper. Humans in the workplace are just workhorses, and toxic leadership prevails. So then, to "expect the unexpected" is hardly around. However, the unexpected – black swan events, do visit us one day, the day of disastrous outcomes. Long sleepy volcanoes do erupt one day. Humans aren't programmed to be ever ready to meet risky moments; boredom and fatigue of prolonged periods of non-observance of disastrous events make people sleepy. However, risk never sleeps.

Given the fact that black swan events would occur, the question is how to deal with it. Are there strategies to be of any help? How to be prepared for large-impact and hard to forecast events? Despite the double hull and other unsinkable features of the Titanic ship, the liner did sink. In engineering, minor events that never get counted into designing often become the cause of disastrous happenings. For instance, electric wiring became the cause of one big plane falling from the skies; a gas cylinder leak caused the 22-story building in England, robustly designed, to fall to grounds. A small trigger leads to consequential outcomes. It would seem nothing helps black swan events, then why bother. However, risk avoidance strategies do help. After the hazard has taken place, after the hurricanes and tornadoes have left destruction behind, immediate acts of rescue and restoration do help. In the USA Federal organization exists (FEMA), and it helps people in restoring lives. However, instances are plenty when such existence failed to help.

The strategy of redundancy is a promising idea, too. Strategy based on regulations helps risk avoidance. For instance, gun controls wherever are in place globally, disasters like Sandy Hook are avoidable. Regulatory controls do help to avoid fiscal crisis likes of 2007-2008. India comparatively did well. Self-regulatory ideas seem to succumb to the temptation of humans falling for greed and fear. Risk transfers through insurance help; however, the strategy of risk controls and risk addressed at the time of design of the project seem to be an excellent idea. Risk resilience through redundancy helps efficiently. Well, black swan events would visit us for sure sooner than later. Response preparedness to such events helps to mitigate the disastrous outcomes. It helps both the leadership as well as the people. Failure of leadership on such occasions lead to their ouster only. Organizations and countries go belly up in voids of risk avoidance strategies in place.

According to Publilius Syrus, "Anyone can hold the helm when the sea is calm." However, 'Black Swan' events are when the leadership's grit is put to the test. Leadership is about showing a path during uncertainty; it's about managing crisis; it's about solving people's problems and help to achieve their vision. In the real world, people often hold leadership positions, and things are managed routinely. In most situations in the ordinary course of things, leaders are defined by the positions they hold. But authentic leaders are defined by their ability to innovate and show vision and walk paths that never ever have been trodden before. Crisis and black swan events are the facts of life. A true leader would meet a situation and be with the people. "Be There," leadership in two words works.

Several steps need attention and focus of leadership for crisis management. First, of course, is an adaptive one: just adapt to the new realities. For example, a storm invokes its brutal force and ravages through a city, and leaves destruction behind in no time. It would require an immediate crisis response indeed: locate lives, provide immediate relief -medical, food, and shelter. It's the time to "Be Aware" and to "Be there." Leadership – the state actors, got to have a sense of "how it feels" passing through trauma and left in despair within no time with no fault of their own. Being there helps people as well as the leadership. For example, The President lost no time in visiting the storm's site. He was there. It helped.

Second, it involves coming out of the shock-recovery phase, and extraordinary actions are needed for an extraordinary situation. Invoke on all the financial muscle and engage the community in recovery steps. For example, non-essential businesses were shut down during the pandemic, and all focus turned on medical relief. At the next level, people bounce back: call it a "V" shape recovery or

"K" shape recovery. And finally, a path forward plans for the future events not to be caught unaware again. The thing of everything is that leadership must be transparent during the adaptive and recovery phase; it doesn't necessarily mean that transparency can be slaughtered at the other stages. For instance, during pandemic management in New Zealand, the PM earned great applause in stating and sharing facts with the people for the steps she proposed to take to defeat the monster virus.

On the contrary, in India, transparency of the leadership faced turbulence, and Indian citizens – migrant workers, suffered heavily from the arbitrary decisions of the state actors. The essence of democracy is "Rule of Law" and "Equity." However, unequal facilities were available to different people during the pandemic: people of scanty means suffered disproportionately higher. A pertinent question must be asked, "Are some people the less citizens of the country?" Even during the economic recovery phase, the wealthy reaped high profits, and the "Not-So-Rich" waited in food queues. "Be There" is the only way to lead folks out of the fault line. "Be There," two words tell a tale of authentic leadership.

Planning for such (black swan disastrous events) events would be an idea of any reasonable person interested in solving problems. For example, in India, floods destroy everything that comes their way almost every year in one or the other part of the country. Sometimes, it is Chennai, sometimes, it is Mumbai, and almost regularly, it's Bihar, Odisha, and Assam that face the rage of floods destroying their homes and fields. A warning about the extremity of the flooding in Chennai, for example, at least, would have allowed people to stock enough food and water; it would have provided an opportunity to put the planes in a safer place. But that wasn't the case. The simple point of argument here is that much less funding is needed to put plans in place than it is spent on the rescue and recovery measures. For example, in India (our country), we have yet to delineate the flood plains. How much does it cost? Certainly, less than the destruction value and what we spend on reconstruction. Despite all the well-intentioned best efforts of the government machinery, much could be achieved by planning for such events. Benjamin Franklin said, "If we fail to plan, we plan to fail." It is so valid for black swan events. By just ignoring the application of modern tools like GIS and not getting the flood plains delineated that would make things predictable, we, in fact, are failing to plan and planning to fail again and again. Yes, we have departments to meet emergencies, and the state actors do respond within a reasonable time for rescue measures. Still, the ground realities are different: it takes days to reach spots of events to provide much-needed help. It is like the Katrina event in the USA; response teams' reaction time was much higher than the desirable. It's the canary in the coal mine that we fail to see again and again.

Commons can only be safe if protected. Protection of commons needs investment from regulatory authorities. Investment in technological tools that are available today is much less than the expenditure on the outcome/aftermath of the extreme events that bring about destruction. It's a story of destruction and reconstruction again and again. The question is, why? Why can't we place enough funds for technological tools and for the purpose of flood plains delineation? This would help the predictability of runoff water by knowing how much water falls from the sky, but it would also help our city planning. For example, a city like Panchkula (Haryana, India) that boasts of modern planning is just planned for a 30-50 mm rain. A falling rain equivalent of Chennai would leave these "so-called" planned cities equally vulnerable. It's simple: runoff is not a part of the equation of city planning. We seem to plan, still, fail to plan, and plan to fail. Future planning helps to avoid or, at least, mitigate the onslaught of unexpected events. Yet another example of a planned city, Gurgaon, tells the same tale. A little bit of rain and all roads are full of rain and sewer water. Runoff was never a part of the city planning.

Navigating disruption and uncertainty is an arduous job for a leader. Pandemic 2020 has brought it to the fore and made it more evident than ever before that leaders find themselves in a complex situation to deal with. Humans love certainty and control; however, black swan events make it abundantly clear that control does not take time to slip away. According to Satya Nadella, "know it all; learn it all" mindset works for a leader to handle uncertainty. Hubris, on the other hand, compounds problems and makes situations out of control. For instance, in (2021) handling of the pandemic in India, leadership failed to see the writing on the wall, and chaos landed up – the worst nightmare for the state actors. Accepting facts helps only: extreme events do occur, and planning does help.

****

11

Impactful Leadership

Governing structures exist in one form or other in all the countries. In some countries, republics and democracies thrive; in some countries, authoritarian systems prevail; in some countries, kingdoms exist. Through these governance instruments, people contract with the state actors to preserve and protect their lives, liberty, and property. However, in practice, many people seldom have the right to life, freedom, and protection of their property, especially in authoritarian governance structures. Even in democracies, de facto authoritarian rule prevails. For instance, in many states of the country (India), even though de jure "rule of law" exists, people are hauled up for treason for expressing dissent against the government actors. Isn't it ironic, though, that the state actors who got leadership positions through the democratic process of elections start playing authoritarian? Freedom of speech is the statute; police arrests people invoking treason acts. As a result, people start feeling stifled and fear for their safety.

The marginal sensitivity to the safety of the people increases instead of decreasing. It foretells misery.

Civil service officers are the keystone officers in the ecosystem of governance in India. Keystone species play a crucial role in the functioning of an ecosystem and help define the whole ecosystem. They have an enormous impact on the habitat. It has a disproportionately large effect in making or breaking a structure. Removal of the keystone guarantees the destruction of a structure. From various reports of committees and the write-ups of eminent, uniquely experienced, and highly regarded persons in the service, it is crystal clear that all is not well. Keystones have become fragile and pose a danger to the governance ecosystem. The question is, what do we do? Some solutions have been hinted at by making the personnel accountable for the wrongdoings. The fact of the matter is that officers in the civil service hold key positions. Their decisions make a difference in the lives of the people. And the impact is large. If a decision favors the rule of law, leadership is impactful. However, on the contrary, if a decisiion favors an individual for personal gains, the impact is troublesome. Measuring decisions' and actions' impact on the defined goals helps knowing the performace in the right direction.

If gaps are visible, corrective action kicks in. Impact diamond analysis is one such tool that helps picture's clarity.

MSS

The concept of Marginal Sensitivity to Safety (MSS) is defined as the propensity to fear with the diminishing rule of law. Marginal sensitivity to safety is an incremental safety concern of a person with an increasing crime rate, diminishing democratic institutions, and increasing authoritarianism. MSS is a weighted average of rogue elements into the judiciary, police, and executive instruments. For instance, 6 Jan 2021, in the USA capitol insurrection generated fear among even the people sitting at the helm of affairs. If the lawmakers' lives could be in jeopardy, imagine what could happen to main street people. Without any doubt, people's concern for their safety increases. MSS thus measures the misery of the people. In other words, it can be understood as a misery index as well. As per figure 2.1 (chapter two, Figure 2.1), diminishing the "rule of law" diminishes the income of the people and poses an existential threat. Safety is a part of the economic equation, and the economic equation is a part of the existential equation.

If we reduce MSS, it increases the excellent governance multiplier. The rule of law impacts good governance. A slight increase in the safety of the people and bringing about the expanded rule of law raises the income of the people significantly. Its effect is impactful. On the contrary, if the crime rate increases, it diminishes the income generation of the country multi-fold. It impacts negatively. To increase this multiplier then is the goal of any governance structure in place. Leadership at the time is solely and squarely responsible for the miserable conditions of the people for not putting in place the rule of law. Other development factors evaporate in thin air if the crime rate increases, and the state actors become complicit. For, instance in India, as per the NN Vohra's report and views expressed by eminent law and order enforcers (DGP Julio Ribeiro), police, criminals, and politicians are complicit. The outcome is self-evident: poverty.

How to measure MSS and thus measure good governance multiplier is an issue that needs a solution. Impact diamond framework is an additional tool in the toolbox. For "the rule of law," the following institutions/agencies are critical: Judiciary, Police, and General Administration. For instance, the DOJ (Department of Justice) can make or break democratic institutions by upholding the "rule of law" or being loyal to a person at the helm of affairs and ignoring the rule book. Police can be used as a state instrument to intimidate people into making authoritarianism flourish. To reflect upon the performance of these institutions, then, an evaluation framework certainly helps. To achieve this goal, a score is needed on a scale of 1to10, or in percentage terms how effective or rotten the institutions are.

The police is an agency that is responsible for implementing the rule of law. Its functioning is critical. So is the case with the judiciary. The state's executive that carries out the state's policies is responsible for the corruption, nepotism, and cronyism in the governance ecological system. Understanding governance as an ecological equilibrium is a way forward. Executive heads or the officers in positions are the keystones in the governance ecological structure. If any keystone malfunctions, the structure becomes fragile. On a positive note, if keystone officers are pro democratic institutions, even though the head of the state is authoritarian, the governance structure sustains the fault line turbulence.

Impact Diamond

There is no physical instrument to measure the performance of social parameters like a barometer that measures air pressure. However, in social systems, a survey is a useful tool. For example, one hundred people were randomly selected from a pool of executives, judicial officers, civil servants, police officers, and people of local eminence from the public, and their best guess figures were obtained. Average was calculated for each parameter. Then came the question of weights to the parameters: each parameter certainly is not of equal weight. This question has been dealt with reasonable assumptions of reasonable people. Accordingly, a weight of 30% each has been assigned to the judiciary, police. 20% weight goes to corruption issues, and 10% each has been assigned to nepotism and cronyism. $\sum P_i*X_i$ formula came in handy to reach the weighted average. The reader can exercise his or her prudence and reach his or her own conclusions. The essence, however, remains the same: Improvement in the rule of law guarantees an increase in income of the people and thus prosperity. It reflects upon the governance multiplier as well. Benefits increase or decrease by tweaking each parameter. For instance, in the case of Haryana, an improvement in the police performance by a factor of 20%, governance multiplier increases from 1.8 to 2.5. This is lots. The results are consistent with Amnesty international surveys and justice Markandey Katju's opinion. For instance, the corruption figure worked out to be 60%, more or less consistent with the global amnesty survey.

Similarly, other parameters can be focused upon, and the multiplier effect would be visible. Often, we hear good governance. But what is good governance? I would put it this way: if a multiplier of 4 and above (or even three and above) is reached, it's good governance; otherwise, it's just propaganda. A computer application (leadershipgov.com) has been developed for this simple calculation, and the user can plug in the best guess numbers and self-see the governance multiplier. This application does speak about the misery index as well. The idea is that what gets measured gets done.

According to the second law of thermodynamics, total input energy is never available for valuable work. This is measured in terms of entropy. In other words, there is a dissipation of energy; there is a wastage of resources; there is a cost of doing business. The question is, how much is available for the valuable work? In governance, too, there is entropy. The goal is to reduce entropy and make resources available for useful work as efficiently as possible. There would be reactance losses; however, reducing reactance is the objective of avoiding heavy losses. In the electricity delivery system power factor measures the actual power available for the useful work. Power factor (for a math interested person, it is $Cos(\phi)$, and we have $Cos(\phi)$ meters to measure the power factor) is less than one. This means reactive power has taken away its share from the pool of electricity that was made available to the system. For heavy machinery, reactance load is comparatively higher, and thus power factor is lower. Electricity people, however, are bright and add to the power factor for billing purposes. It's because electricity is lost in reactive terms at the factory level. The electricity department is entitled to charge for the electricity they have made available at the factory gate.

Well, that's all science. For a non-science person to understand, it simply means there is a dissipation of resources along the way. The question is how much is reasonable, how much is not reasonable for effective governance structures to keep people moving. If MSS is 80%, it's miserable. The governance multiplier is less than two. The good multiplier is four or more. In such a situation, with this knowledge, there is a scope to bring down the rotten part in the parameters with greater weights—for instance, police or judiciary and corruption. Any rotten part reduction in each parameter would help misery go away and allow the governance multiplier to go up.

The idea is that this analysis tool offers an opportunity for strengthening weak points and working on solutions. It's one of the tools in the analysis toolbox. And the fact of the matter is that 100% performance is an impossibility like in the physics law of entropy. It offers an understanding of how a system functions. There are attritions along the way and should be accepted as such. Understanding governance as an ecosystem and relating its functions with natural laws tell us about that deviation from natural laws is dangerous and poses an existential threat.

Figure 11.1

Governance Impact Diamond

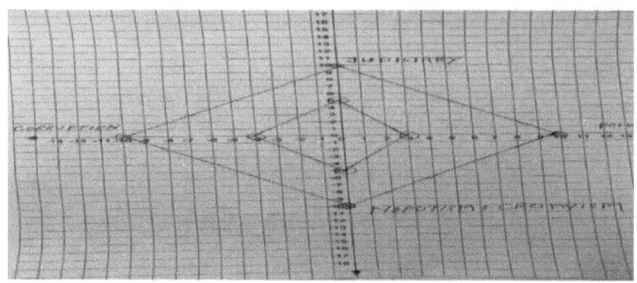

In figure 11.1, impact diamond analysis, the useful work accomplished by the state actors is depicted by the inner diamond. The bigger diamond is an ideal situation where input energy is converted into 100% useful work. However, that is not the case because the system uses resources during the conversion process. The area between the outer diamond and the inner diamond is governance entropy. This means these resources are not available for useful work. The takeaway point is that the entropy area must be minimized, and the inner diamond area needs to be maximized. Good governance would always make efforts to reduce the governance entropy and increase the useful work done so that the people prosper and are safe. This is what authentic leadership would do: reduce corruption, improve the justice system, improve police functioning, and minimize nepotism and cronyism. A 10% reduction in the rotten percentage in each area would result in a multiplier of 2.08 instead of 1.72. The improved inner diamond depicts this in figure 11.2.

Similarly, if we reduce the rotten part again by another 10%, it's remarkable to see that the governance multiplier increases to almost 3. This means what the government does, its impact is three times. Isn't it great to reduce the rotten stuff a bit and get many-fold benefits to the people?

Figure 11. 2

Governance Impact Diamond (10% Entropy reduction)

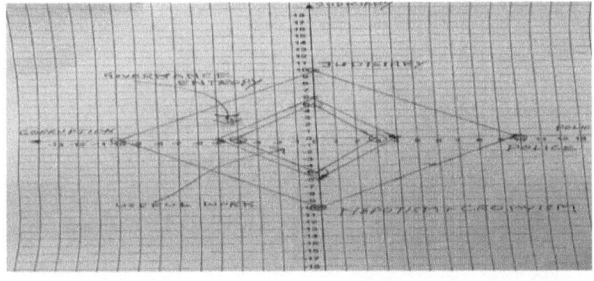

In figure 11.2, impact diamond analysis, it is an impact of reducing the rotten stuff by just 10%. We can mitigate defective stuff more easily until we reach an inner diamond area up to 80 % of the outer diamond. In this scenario, the governance multiplier would be 5. It means excellent work done by the government would result in five times benefits (five times impact) to the people. This would be a desirable thing to do. It simply means a decent work done gets reflected in 5 other good works. However, even we allow governance entropy of 25%. Still, it's an outstanding achievement. Indeed, it deserves to be called good governance. In this scenario, a multiplier of 4 is in operation, which is good enough. The problem is that this is not the case in reality. As per the experts' best guess estimates, the multiplier is currently less than 2, which is dismal. The Miserability level is approximately 70%. This means 70% of the people are struggling with their lives: they are worried about employment; they are concerned about good schooling for their kids; they are worried about health facilities available to them; to top it all, they are worried about their safety.

The fact of the matter is that mechanism has not been put in place, and the warnings have not been heeded. Some state actors land up in jail after prolonged trials; however, the situation has not changed much. If the Mumbai recent revealings (2021, Home minister asking IPS officers for collecting tributes in large numbers from extortion of small business people) are any evidence, the rot has gone deep down and increased. Adarsh Society apartments story is another evidence about the top-down rotten stuff the country's people live with. It's more than clear that the rot exists. The question is how to remove it? Or, at least, reduce it? My take on this is that offices of DM and SSP of the districts be restructured with the responsibility and accountability of both as one team, as one body, DM being the chair. Measure the team's performance on the scale of "Rule of Law." If the rule of law is taken care of, everything else falls in place. If people worry for their safety, economic costs (to the system as a whole) rise multifold. The following narrative explains a lot.

    Nand Kishore Sharma was busy with his 10-year-old-bicycle fixing it. "Why don't you buy a new one? I will pay for it," I asked. He said, "Money isn't the issue. The real issue is that someone will steal the new one. So old, nobody looks at." "I got to visit Mandi (market) almost every day to buy daily need stuff, and I got to park it. I can't keep an eye on it and do my shopping at the same time." Humph...," I murmured. Then I wondered why people would steal a bicycle in this city. Well, there are people still who don't have bikes (bicycles) and need one, I thought. I thought it could be because of the city's poor law and order situation that people don't feel safe parking their bikes at the marketplace and fear someone will steal them. The thought took me to the economic question of how poor law and order situations affect economic activity. A new bicycle missed sales costs a businessperson as lost revenue. Economic costs, though, are much higher. Two things stand out here: first, if he buys a new bike, his productivity will undoubtedly increase. Second, he can sell the old one, and someone could buy it at a much lower price and improve their productivity. Not only this but a new bike would also be produced at the factory. That would add to the economy in terms of employment. Suppliers of raw material to the factory would produce more, and wages paid to the employees would equip them to buy more products from the market. This would set in a chain of economic multipliers. But a scary law and order situation applies a break on this phenomenon.

Another similar encounter I had with a businessperson who had a small oil mill and warehouses for renting. He was delighted to show his success in his business in such a brief time. As we were walking around the place, he said, "I have this additional space and would construct two more warehouses of bigger size than the existing one." "Great," I said. I added, "It's the right thing to scale up as credit conditions are favorable." "No, no, no. Not right now. I will wait a bit and then expand. It's because government agencies start looking around, and it invites trouble," he added hastily. "Why should the government agencies create any trouble when you are helping the economy to grow during this slow time?" I asked. He explained that people look for something and aren't bothered by more significant issues. I sensed how corruption could impact growth. "If he is free of things non-relevant to his business, he would immediately invest his own money, take credit from a bank, and expand", I thought. His expanded business would generate employment. However, the fear of interfering authorities created trouble in his mind, and the genuine business activity got stymied because of the poor governance. Imagine, if his business activity goes ahead, it will generate direct employment in the warehouse, and he would get rent that he would pay for his credit back. And some profit left to be invested later. The suppliers of the material for the construction of the warehouse would benefit because of their business going up. And thus, the economic chain of activities results. It's not only the direct one business activity, but several related business activities take off. In addition to employment generation, it adds to the consumption of goods that further adds to the economic growth. In plain words: if an environment of fear exists, it generates entropy, and a multiplier effect of economic growth is missed. Governance entropy thus isn't great support, rather a drag on the economic system. It blocks economic growth, and it stops multi times – the multiplier effect. Law and order is a necessary condition for the economy to grow. This is what this conversation with a businessperson depicts.

Yet another interaction with another businessperson tells the same story. The gentleman was one of the top guys of the city – doing financially well and having good business. One day we agreed to assess the potential of an area in the region. It was decided we would go in his private car and un-noticed and as usual customers. We did the assigned job and were ready to have some food. During the conversation, a conversation about the latest cars in the market popped out. I asked, "Why don't you buy the latest swanky car when you have lots of money at your disposal?". He kept silent for a while and then said, "Well, buying a car is not an issue; the issue is: am I going to use it?" He advanced an example of businesspeople in Pakistan who don't generally buy big and swanky cars, instead keep a low profile, and drive secondhand cars because of fear of new vehicles getting stolen. I said, "India is not Pakistan." He said, "Yes, but politicians do create trouble." In this story, too, the same fear is depicted, and well-deserved consumption is missed. In the economic context, consumption defines growth. And it has Keynesian multipliers. "Rule of Law" indeed has a tremendous impact on economic activities of a country. If "Rule of Law" is efficient, it generates a good economy and lifts people above the poverty level by generating employment. If the country's people are poor, it's because the state actors aren't doing their job: Fair and square.

****

12

Assessing Leadership

The human brain is wired to assess. After receiving a clue from the environment, it automatically does the calculus of wrong and right. It assesses the pros and cons and then executes the decision, which appears to be the best out of the alternatives. People have the right to assess their leaders and know if they are performing as they promised. The leaders are required to come up to the expectations. Organizations spend a lot of money and energy to assess and correct course. In personnel management systems, employees are assessed on performance standards. In corporations, leaders are assessed on shareholders' value creation. Sometimes, the bottom line targets are used as narrow indicators.

Leadership assessment essentially involves how people feel in general: do they feel hurt; do they feel short on promises made; do they feel happy about things? For example, people were happy with Bill Clinton's economic well-being. "It's the economy, stupid" (phrase coined by James Carville in 1992, Bill Clinton's strategist) became the assessment baseline. Individual existential security lies in collective security, and that's why we live in cities and villages in groups. In the civilized world, the rule of law is preferred to be in line with this ideation. If one breaks a rule, which is gainful to an individual, but painful to the collective existence, the person is held accountable. If leaders fail to be consistent with the Rule of Law, how to hold them accountable is the question. To know the leaders' performance, assessing them on the parameters that are consistent with the rule of law is the right thing to do. If we know it, we can tell them and ask them to correct the course.

Self-assessment is a tool, which practitioners and government agencies can use for good governance. It offers insights in assessing opportunities and risks. Historically, the minority gets organized, and the unorganized majority continues to suffer. For the majority to have some semblance of organization and keep the violators within boundaries, evaluating the minority on well-defined parameters is a promising idea. For example, governance could be assessed on the parameters of the rule of law, corruption, nepotism, cronyism, and justice delivery. People don't have a barometer to gauge the pressure, but they feel where it hurts. By asking people where exactly it pains, we can have a device to measure and assess the leadership.

Natural laws govern the universe's existence. Scientific thought has served humankind. Scientific laws are tried and tested in theory and in labs. We, therefore, can use the scientific laws as tools in solving governance and social ecosystem issues, including assessing our leaders. In the following narrative, the laws of the natural sciences of entropy and domino effect are presented as useful in understanding, analyzing, and solving socio-economic ecosystem problems and assessing governance. There can be 'n' numbers of scientific tools that can be pressed into service and solve problems. The idea is that using tools based on known nature's laws provides us additional insights.

The notion of Entropy

Entropy is about disorder and randomness. According to the second law of thermodynamics, the total system's heat is not available for the intended outcome. Some heat is lost in increasing entropy. Can we understand social systems in terms of physical and natural systems? If yes, can we apply the methods of analysis of physics and nature's laws to study and analyze social systems? Application of physics and nature's laws to understand a social system is insightful. Entropy is one concept that has its origin in physics. In the electricity flow, reactance is not available for useful work. In heat systems, the energy, which is not available, we call it entropy. In social systems, it is analogous to the inefficiency of inputs. The power factor (and hence loss as reactance) is measured by a $Cos(\phi)$ meter in the physical world. However, in social systems, we cannot use such instruments of physicality.

Nevertheless, measurement of entropy is possible in social systems as well. The survey method is one. For instance, the rule of law is measurable in terms of crime rate. A corruption index is possible by way of a survey. If we can reach a figure of entropy in percentage terms, we can do other calculations. It helps in knowing and understanding losses. As we know, zero entropy is an impossibility; the idea is then to minimize the non-useful work energy and thus, maximize the valuable work.

The notion of entropy can be applied to good governance. It is possible to calculate governance entropy by scoring on indicative performance parameters. For example, we can use the following guidelines to understand a social system's entropy. Ignorance in governance would be highly damaging and thus inefficient. We can easily say ignorance means total entropy.

Similarly, uncertainty is entropy. Information, and transparency, on the other hand, decrease entropy. Perfect market competition would be zero entropy (but an impossibility like a perfect market is an impossibility). Similarly, no reactance in electricity flow means no entropy or Power factor is 100%. Again, this is an impossibility. We can say that zero entropy is a non-reality. In electricity, the power factor is measured as $\cos(\phi)$. Thus, entropy would be equal to $1 - \cos(\phi)$. It is on the same pattern as in heat engines, where some heat or energy is not available for useful work. In the electricity flow process, a part of electricity gets lost in reactance and thus, not available for useful work. Analogously, in the governance ecosystem, there exists a phenomenon of entropy. As in physical systems, in governance systems, too, we can measure it; we can identify the gaps, find solutions, and help good governance.

The notion of Domino Effect

In physics, it has been observed that a domino has potential energy and when it falls on the next domino, its impact energy is higher than the energy required to topple it down. The knock-on effect is one and a half times taller than the falling domino. In other words, a falling domino can knock down the next domino of 1.5 times the height of the falling domino. It's energy amplification. Continuing the process, the next domino would have the knock-on effect of 1.5 times on the next domino. For instance, if the first domino is one meter, it would knock down the next domino of 1.5 meters height, and the second domino would have the amplified force enough to knock down the third one of the height of 2.25 meters (1.5 times 1.5) and so on. If we apply this natural science principle to social sciences, an evil deed will result in many bad outcomes with dangerous existential issues.

On the contrary, a good act would result in amplified benefits to the social ecosystem, and progress would take place. The multiplier effect is observable as in the case of entropy as well. If we reduce the entropy of the social systems to keep them in equilibrium, the consequential effects are in multiples of the original act. In the words of Ralph Waldo Emerson, it's the ripple effect, and the impact is wide – "Throw a stone into the stream and the ripples that propagate themselves are the beautiful type of all influence."

Assessing Governance

Governance entropy can be defined as the governance energy not available for valuable work to the people. The work of the state actors, which is not available to the people, can be used to measure governance entropy. The fact of the matter is that it is not a one-time entropy event; its impact is multi times. To assess the actual impact multiplier, assessment is necessary. It's like a Keynesian multiplier for an investment and the resultant effect of multi times. The governance multiplier can be calculated by dividing one by entropy on the same pattern as calculating the money multiplier by dividing one by the reserve ratio. The question is how to know the governance entropy. Governance is not a natural science; however, natural laws can be applied to understand, and entropy is one such analysis tool that can be used to know governance impact. The idea of a multiplier is to focus on the point that one good act results in so many other good acts through a chain-linked action.

In figure 12.1, There are five domain indicators that have been taken into consideration for the assessment of the governance: Police, Judiciary, Corruption, Nepotism, and Cronyism. The score on each variable is used to calculate the entropy of the governance as an administrative ecosystem. As has been amply evidenced by research, the rule of law is positively correlated with economic wellbeing. In other words, better law and order situation increases confidence among people to do business, which generates employment, and people spend wages to buy products. Spending defines economic growth. This is like a chain: one activity triggers another, and economic gains are spread far and wide. Police dealings with the people and judiciary outcomes define the rule of law. Corruption in the system is another drag that holds back business activities and missed economic opportunities. So is the case with Nepotism and Cronyism.

A weighted average score on all these variables is the entropy of the entire system. Figure 12.1, computer application does all the work after the figures are filled in.

It is based upon the best estimations of the people who perceive the police as rotten (inefficient, problematic), how the judiciary succeeds in delivering justice, and the prevalence of corruption in the governance system. It's the confidence that people have in the governance system that motivates them to act or not to act. Knowing is the hard part; rest is downhill. If we know the rot, it can be eliminated or at least reduced to a reasonable level. According to natural sciences laws, it is impossible to have zero entropy. In the governance system, too, some energy is inevitably wasted as the inefficiency of governance.

The thing is that there is a cost of doing business. The question is, how much? 10%, 20% or 50%? If 50%, it's a red signal. 10 to 20 would be acceptable as zero is an impossibility.

Figure 12.1 (leadershipgov.com)

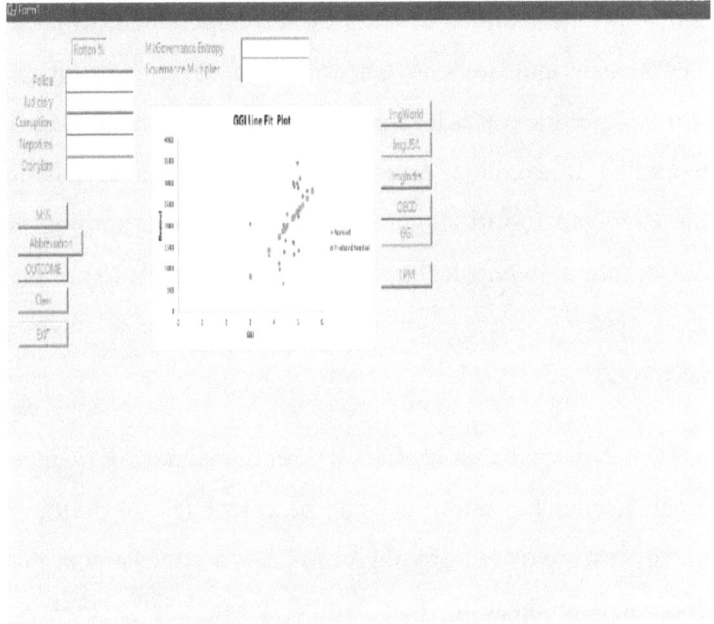

Assessing Leaders

An analysis tool similar to the governance entropy can be applied to estimate leadership entropy. State actors are the keystones in the administrative ecosystem's structure of a country. An authentic leader delivers better results and hence less entropy into the system. A terrible act can create turbulence then how to know that a leader would handle a situation that requires great care. Leaders do have traits and dispositions in addition to temperament to lead. Ten domain indicators have been identified for measuring a leaders' abilities. If a leader outstands these capabilities, it would be an excellent probability for the leader to deliver the expected results. It's a probability because nothing is 100% sure as in physical systems; it is impossible to use the total system's energy for useful work. There is always entropy.

Nevertheless, it offers a direction and a confidence level. Leadership multiplier can be calculated by dividing one by a score on entropy. Figure 12.2 is a screenshot of the computer application that would be a useful tool to calculate. There are ten domain indicators that have been taken into consideration for the assessment of leaders, as mentioned above.

Parameters that affect the entropy of Leadership (Leadership Productivity Multiplier Factors)

- Ignorance (Non-awareness, Training deficit, networking deficit, Chhattisgarh DM)
- Inertia (inaction, not doing or avoiding a situation is not an option).
- Hubris (self-aggrandizement, there are others)

- Empathy (Be there, don't humiliate, make them feel two inches taller)
- Transparency (share it with the people and explain why – Pandemic New Zealand PM)
- Ethics (do the right thing, integrity).
- Authentic leadership (not positional – it's about the people, not about you. DM's behavior)
- Dilemma (There is only one lemma – loyal to rule book, Rule of Law, Instinct vs. intelligence)
- Fire Within (fire of doing something, no slow down)
- Initiative (Innovative methods, initiate a project - successor won't have a choice – Library)

Figure 12.2 (leadershipgov.com)

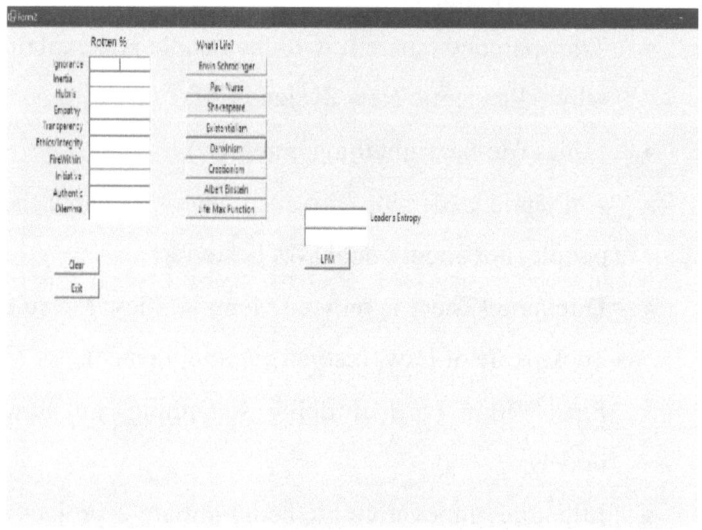

In figure 12.2, a leader's performance is scored on the given ten parameters to calculate entropy. Ignorance carries the highest weight. If an individual is ignorant of ignorance of his own ignorance, they are unfit to lead. Blind spots must be known; a leader is supposed to be aware of what they are dealing with. Unfortunately, leaders are seldom aware of their own toxicity.

Research has evidenced the fact that subordinate officers suffer more anxiety as compared to senior officers. Is it the financial anxiety only? Or the toxicity of the senior leadership has something to do with it? Well, as presented in Figure 12.3, a screenshot of another computer application, the toxicity of a leader is measurable, too. It's based upon Hare's scale of psychopathy. If a leader scores high on the psychopathy scale, toxicity is extremely high. It indicates a leader who only seems to care for themselves, and personal gains matter more than peoples' concerns. For instance, an Oxford University psychiatry professor found that President Trump scored extremely high on this scale, more or less, as Hitler scored on this scale. Toxic leaders cannot be put in the category of authentic leadership. They are not there for the people, and seldom are they aware of it. A score on this scale over 30 indicates sociopathy. If such a person finds a high leadership place, people will live with pain and penury. A leader can self-assess and improve upon by being aware of the self-toxins.

Figure12.3 (leadershipgov.com)

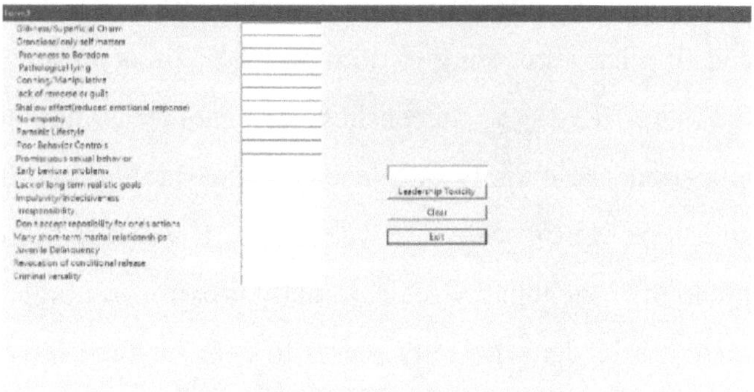

Insights From Pandemic Experience

Pandemic turned the whole universe topsy turvy. Lots of disorder. In other words, lots of entropy. One small invisible (2020, 2021) microbe brought the entire world to a halt. The illusion of control and certainty got shattered. Consequently, people perceived it as if their life and liberty had been snatched as a consequence of lockdowns and shutdowns. President of the USA Trump said, "People want their life back." Finally, vaccines appeared, and vaccination took off. After that, life started to come back to normal. However, countries without vaccination facilities still face problems. During this phase of pandemic, economic costs to humanity shot up in addition to the lives lost. People lost jobs, students lost their academic years, and businesses got shut down. For instance, in quarter one of the year 2020, GDP fell by 24.4% (-24.4%) in India. For the year overall 2020, the rate is negative 7.3%. The unemployment rate increased to 7.11%. As per CMEI estimation, the figure unemployment is approx. 15%. The most noticeable thing that happened during this pandemic rage is about inequalities: unequal treatment was meted out to the people by the state actors; inequal medical facilities were available to different people; financial inequalities increased as the pandemic raged on.

During the adaptive phase, during the recovery phase, during the resilience phase, and moving forward, every time, the upper section of society benefited disproportionately compared to the lower section of the society in economic terms. As a result, the entropy of the system increased. It all started with chaos – more disorder as the unknowns of the virus swirled around. Lockdowns of economies were without forethought and foretelling people. Non-transparency increased entropy. Uncertainty among the people added to the panic and thus added to the entropy of the governance. State actors acted ignorantly and increased entropy: washing migrant laborers with disinfectants, beating people on the roads, and allowing the top politicians to hold rallies and parties. Remember that increase in the social system's entropy results in lowering the multiplier effect.

Different countries acted differently. Some countries used data as a guiding force for policy decisions, and some countries weren't as transparent as some successful countries were. For example, Singapore continuously and consistently kept its people informed and did better. Evidence-based policy is the hallmark of good governance. There has not to be a tradeoff between inequality and growth. Countries with greater transparency and with data-based policy did better. Greater transparency reduces entropy in the governance system. On the contrary, opaque decisions making serves only the people who care for personal gains. In the state of MP, India, there was a transparency problem, and substandard hospitals opened shops to make money at the cost of the Covid 19 fear-stricken people.

Pandemic tested leadership all over the globe. Some countries excelled in handling, and some countries did not do so well. Different setups of circumstances in each country played a role. However, leaders who were consistently transparent with their people did comparatively better. It can take a long time to recover from tough times. There have been policy shifts. High-pressure distributional benefits have become part of public policy. High-pressure distributional benefits necessarily need not be high inflationary. The goal is to deal with the virus, mitigate damages done (avoid scarring). Fiscal response goals included relieving the hardships people faced as a consequence of job losses. Fiscal stimulus should be enough to restore aggregate demand to pre-pandemic levels. However, some countries have fiscal constraints.

The question is how long it will take for the millions to get their jobs back. Will it be a V shape recovery, or will it be a K shape recovery? So far, evidence suggests that it is a K shape recovery, and governance acts have benefitted the rich more than the people who stood to lose everything because of a pandemic. Inequalities have increased, and wealthy people benefited. There has been a zero-bound problem since the 1990s. As a consequence, fiscal policy has become less costly. This gives confidence for providing good stimulus money. Some countries have responded well. For instance, the USA, Finland, Sweden, Singapore, and some other countries' fiscal response was more than 20% of GDP. It helped recovery measures. During the pandemic, one thing that stands out is: talking straight to the people and defining things as clearly as possible lowers the entropy of the governance system. Being there with the people in uncertain times is a good leadership strategy.

****

13

Leadership & Winning Strategies

The journey of leadership is as arduous and full of rough and tumble as the journey of life. If life is understood as a moment in time and space, so is leadership. Leadership is complex, dynamic, and contextual. A successful leader in business may necessarily not succeed in political settings. A war hero may not excel in peace times. A leader of yesteryears might not appreciate the aspirations of the modern-day generation. In leadership training classes, very often, cliché loaded discourses are delivered. For example, "set your priorities right, the customer is the king, the rule of law must be abided by, follow the constitution, hold the wrongdoers accountable, the steel frame has become rusty, police & politicians are complicit, and we need to change course," are the staple academic stuff. In management classes and later as a trainee officer at Mussoorie academy, we heard it again and again.

The thing is that it hasn't ended even after so many years of service. My retired colleagues, now experts on the subject of administration and the rule of law, by virtue of long years of experience in leading the forces responsible for upholding the rule of law, and holding the responsible constitutional positions, repeat the same old tales of human rights violations, corruption, cronyism, nepotism, failed law and order situations. Fuzzy notions of loyalty, accountability, vision, teamwork, and so on have not taken us far. If it hasn't worked, then do leaders have strategies in their toolbox to hold promise?

One thing is clear that people are concerned about the sinking efficiency of civil services and the leadership at the time. It is also clear that leadership is crucial in making or breaking things. Sociologically, according to Herbert Spencer, people make leaders before they remake a society. Scientifically, leaders are the keystone species in the governance ecological system. Their actions' impact is large in building or destroying the biome we all exist in. The question is, what can enlightened leadership do to correct course? What strategies do they adopt to win the war?

Successful leaders have applied some strategies, and observable pattern after pattern can be of help.

For example, the pattern of clarity of message is visible. During emergency surgery, the doctors and the nurses all speak the same language. A SWAT team speaks the same language. Every person on the team, with precision, appreciates what their actions mean. Any wrong communication means people die. During the pandemic, leaders with transparent and clear messages had winning strategies. If the leaders – the state actors (civil servants) are clear about what needs to be done, and if the brief is clear, the probability of chaos and sinking into failure gets reduced significantly.

Look in the Eye and Talk Straight

In India, road traffic chaos is not a surprising event. People somehow are used to navigating through red-green lights even in the absence of electricity. Likewise, expecting traffic from the wrong side is not an unexpected event. However, when a chief minister visits a city, people behave, and everything seems to be in order – no traffic chaos.

Why? Simple: brief is clear. People act and the administration conducts. Both are high on transparency. And once the visit is over, routine descends back.

The shock therapy decisions and rapid speed policies are communication stressed. For example, in India, the demonetization policy was announced, sending shock waves down the supply lines. Economy suffered. "The RBI's concern that costs of demonetization will outweigh benefits was conveyed to the government. RBI offered an opinion on alternative approaches to note ban," Rajan said. And still, the expert advice was ignored. He further added that the Committee that took a decision was never communicated to the RBI. As a consequence, both formal and informal economies suffered prohibitive costs. Clear communication about the goalposts, why the actions are being taken, and the likely outcome of achieving the objectives is necessary for a smooth ride.

Yet another example of the absence of clear communication: the sudden lockdown was declared during the pandemic. The outcome was no good: migrant laborers ran on foot to their homes. Out of ignorance, senior IAS officers took and implemented decisions that have no scientific basis – far away from the known facts. It wasn't that they were doing it for pleasure or out of mal intentions; it was just ignorance. Disinfectant machines that sprouted around the country and migrant people were washed with chemicals could not be supported by any reasonable person of knowledge, much less by the scientists. The "so-called disinfectants" – chemicals, cause cancer. When scientists raised their voices, machines were dismantled. Such is the enormity of dangerous outcomes when communication is not clear. People lose lives. For authentic leadership, a clear communication strategy – being on the same page with the people, is a promising strategy.

It's not only in India in many other countries, too; leadership fell short on telling people what the government was up to and why. They fell short on telling people that it was necessary to solve a problem and the method they were using was the best possible method to handle it. Instead, things remained opaque, and people suffered. On the contrary, Singapore, New Zealand,

Taiwan, and many other countries transparently talked to the people and effectively handled the crisis. The point is: Clarity of message and transparency is a good and a winning strategy to lead people. Shock and awe strategy might have meaning against the enemy in a war zone, but not for the people you lead.

Yet another instance is of election times in the democracies that create lots of entropy in communication. Government dignitaries stop taking essential decisions in the absence of who will win and what policies will go under transformation. And after the government formation, the transfer industry consumes quite a time. During this reasonable long-lasting phase of uncertainty, it causes entropy in terms of unclear ambiance. High entropy means low performance and low useful work. Looking in the eye and talking straight with the people helps. If you can't communicate the end goal to the people, you possibly cannot take them aboard. Two-way communication is effective. Passing orders and sending them down the line for implementation leaves so much unfinished.

Authentic leaders take people's concerns and listen to them. In an organization, front-line workers are the best people to suggest solutions. Toyota's Model of leading has been appreciated a lot. It's because it is not a top-down model. Front-line workers play a significant role in continuous improvement and suggesting solutions to the problems. It is the front-line worker who knows the best about the issues and even about the solutions. Their involvement in the identification of the problem and its solution holds great promise. This is what the Toyota model has done, and other organizations seem to take pride in applying this strategy to solve problems. By asking teams on the front line and involving them for solutions, leaders have significant leverage. Asking a question and eliciting answers is an inquiry-driven method for solving problems. Authentic leaders play a game of clear communication as a winning strategy.

Build Teams

Great leaders surround themselves with competent and excellent people of repute. They build exceptional teams and task them to deliver. Persons join civil services and big organizations with a fire in them; they come to make a difference. In the civil services in India, district posting is the position of leadership. The DM-SP team, which the people of a city or a town look upon to solve their problems and express their concerns, holds a crucial leadership position. They are the agent of the government at the time. Through this agency, the government implements its policies, and through their feedback, new policies are developed and replicated if found helpful in other parts of the state or the country.

By taking responsibility and focusing on the facts and the law, they lead the district administration toward the collective goals. In civil services, it is the part of the culture to stand by the oath of loyalty to the constitution and not to an individual – a minister or a chief minister. Once in a while, things go under stress, and civil servants suffer the irrational rage of the elected elite. Nevertheless, all the civil service people of right concerns stand and support such an upright officer. Culture in civil services refers to the general environment of working and the pro rule of law. Culture is about expectations. For instance, people expect the right course of action from the DC-SP team if a disaster event or a situation goes wrong, and law and order go out of hand. Honesty, integrity, and moral uprightness are the perceived hallmark of civil servants, and with pride, they display and serve people. Civil service people associate their performance as a team, as a service, as a cadre. Any singular aberration is taken with concern. People expect just actions from these officers. Such is the culture and faith that has developed over time.

But facts on the ground aren't quite as the expectations. The fellow members of the service have characterized the so-called steel frame as rusty and dysfunctional. Bureaucracy, police, and other departments do not seem to work as a team. As a result, it's not uncommon to see the apparent DM-SP tension in the open. Turf wars aren't unusual.

As a consequence, the rule of law suffers. Adarsh society example as advanced by Vinod Rai in his book is an apparent failure of the system. Bureaucracy, police, politicians complicity does not speak pro-constitution and pro-democratic institutions. Personal gains seemed to have taken precedence over teamwork and pro-democratic institution goals. Playing solo and putting personal goals first isn't a good leadership strategy. In the long run, many people do land up in trouble and aren't heard anymore. My position on the district functioning is this: DC-SP works as a team, as one body. The success of the team is an individual's success. If the team fails, both fail. Communicating effectively with the public by the team and the top leadership that it is the team that is in charge offers excellent leverage for democratic institutions. Civil service culture lies not in holding positions, but it lies in meeting the expectation of the people. And make no mistake, there is no letter 'I' in the word 'Team.' It's an excellent strategy to be surrounded by competent people who are transparent and honest in stating facts to the leadership. Sequacious, sycophants and head-nodding people for everything, a leader says, are trouble.

In a toxic working environment, it becomes difficult to communicate with leaders. They do not wish to hear what they don't like to. Officers, survival as a strategy, speak only what pleases them. This is a dangerous strategy. It would not set them free of their stress in performing their work. The fact of the matter is that despite being toxic in dealings, a leader does not like to lose. It would be in their interest to know the truth on the ground, and it is in the self-interest of the officer to speak the truth without the perceived fear of reprisal. Leaders wish to survive, and when guided and told boldly, they appreciate.

Define Goals and Be on the Same Page

If you can dream it, you can think about it; if you can think about it, you can plan it; if you can plan it, you can set goals; if you can set goals, you can define them; if you can define them, you can communicate them; if you can communicate them, you can measure them; if you can measure them, you can apply diagnostics and adopt the corrective course. Half the problem is solved by clearly defining the goals and communicating transparently. Setting realistic goals makes sense. It is not uncommon to have leaders set goals for their employees based on past trends and predicting beyond practical limits. They tell the employees to achieve the results, and reward and recognition would work on the target achieved. In this scenario, the focus is on the target, and the employees seem to be out of the equation. A leader forgets that they are dealing with people and not objects. If the goals are too high and every time the leader reviews and pushes for the target without feedback as to the bottlenecks, it creates a toxic working environment. For instance, a leader who sets up a goal in a bank and neglects the culture of serving its clients would surely lose them. A good leader would define and communicate visions and goals to its employees clearly and effectively. They communicate without ambiguities. Reviews are held as diagnostics and not as punitive opportunities.

On the contrary, some leaders in governance, holding high office positions, often lead by intimidation as a strategy and pollute the administrative ambiance with toxins of psychopathy. This strategy may bring about results in the short run, but it is not a good strategy in the long run. Research has shown that employee-focused strategies are winning strategies and productive.

Leadership lies in showing the goalposts as clearly as possible and making it clear as to where the role of leadership fits in. Authentic leaders do not use employees as objects to be used for personal credits. Instead, goals and targets are achieved as a team led by the leaders.

It was the part of the assignment - university library computerization; I visited neighboring libraries to brush up on the latest. I visited Punjab University and a college in Punjab as what work has already been accomplished at their library. An MP (member Parliament) had inaugurated the computerization project of the Punjab University. I was curious to visit and learn. On visiting Punjab university, I was informed that just four PCs were made available. It was disheartening to know that it could be anything but computerization. The computerization of a library means many PCs with internet facilities for the students as a common learning center. Then I visited the college library in Amritsar. I requested the in charge to take me around the computer labs and how they accomplished the library's computerization. He pointed toward one PC next to his desk, and he said that they had put all the information about all the books in this PC, and this is computerization.

Again, the goal of computerization was not well defined and well understood, much less clearly communicated to the persons responsible for it. They expressed ignorance as the library's computerization means providing at least three to five computer labs with internet facilities where students work with their projects. There is always a trainer to upgrade the students' skills in handling a PC in one lab.

Yet another example of land records digitization (computerization) in the state of Haryana tells the same tale. The Federal government decided to digitize the land records. Haryana, too, got the funds. That was 1990 (approx.). With a fanfare of getting up to date with technology, the project was launched. I got involved with the same project in the year 2003 or so. During the process of understanding the project, its aims and how it would work, and who would pay for the hardware costs and the employees' compensation, I found no clear communication. It was all vague and fuzzy. The only communication that existed and was understood was the computerization of land records. Nothing more. The project was not defined, much less communicated clearly to the officers responsible for its implementation. It took me a year to figure out (it's a bit technical).

The project was defined, made a team of programmers led by Gurpreet Singh Saini. It required domain knowledge and technical skills. Funding was worked out and taken out of the red tape process. Financial Model was developed on user-based charges. The project started to make some sense. After writing millions of code lines, it took another three years to make it functional in the vernacular language. Now the goal was clear and communicated clearly, and the team was clear about what needs to be done and how they were going to be compensated. Everybody was on the same page. Enough funding for PCs and servers was made available. Haryana took a leading role in digitizing land records, and it was rewarding to the team. The idea is that goals need to be realistically and clearly defined. Vague communication is not the right strategy for leadership. Things don't work that way. It was a case of vague understating and vague communication. When the communication became clear and goals were set realistically, the project worked. In governance, it happens because of inertia. This results in lost opportunities and increases economic costs. A good leader would always be transparent in defining the goal and vision and then communicating it clearly for its implementation to take all team members on board. Strategy works.

One of the glaring examples of undefined and uncommunicated goals is the maintenance of law and order in the state of Haryana, as described in Parkash Singh Committee Report on the role of Civil and Police administration during Jat Reservation Agitation (Feb 2016). It was total chaos, and governance entropy touched almost 100%. Police officers left their posts and ran away. Police stations and administrative offices were set on fire. People were criminally handled, and public property was destroyed. What did the leadership do? From the report, it is crystal clear that there was no communication from the office of the Home Secretary of the state. If the Home Secretary of the state is not in charge, then who? It's amazing to see the response of the then Home Secretary to the Committee that operationally he had no control.

Things were managed directly by the CM office. He was out of the picture. If that is the case, it's a classic case of leaders abandoning the goal post. DGP, too, had no answers to the Committee for any defined strategy, much less communication. He never visited front-line positions and did not even have a video conference with the district SPs.

The committee report further relates the dismal picture of the dysfunctional DC-SP team at the district level. Here is a case where leadership did not perform even in silos, much less a team. Officers in the field were left to their own, and chaos prevailed. From figure 13.1, it would appear, it's a Losers' Strategy: low on defining strategy and low on communication. It's quite the opposite of what authentic leadership would do.

FIGURE 13.1

Winning Strategies

Goal Definition High

High on well-defined goals Low on communication **INERTIA**	High on Well-Defined goals High On Communication **WINNERS**
Low on Well-Defined goals Low on Communication **LOSERS**	Low on well-defined goals High on communication **IGNORANT**
CLEAR COMMUNICATION	

In figure 13.1, four boxes depict the outcome of having or not having well-defined goals and clear communication as key strategies. Winning strategies have high scores on well-defined defined goals and a clear-communication scale. For example, say, one of the goals of leadership is the happiness of the people. But what is happiness? Happiness goal got to be defined in clear terms and communicated transparently to the officers for implementation. For example, happiness may be defined as the US $90,000 (PPP equivalent) as income of the households, education, and health standards as defined by the education and health specialists. How to achieve the well-stated income level would require actions. For instance, the Rule of Law is a necessary condition for good income. Then the rule of law parameters got to be defined and acted upon. How it is going to be implemented would further require policy shifts. Will the existing system be able to deliver, or will a system shift, too, require transformation and so on. The fact is that a winning strategy has the essential elements of well-defined goals and clear communication.

Successful leaders know it, and they utilize it. For example, in the state of UP, CM Yogi made the brief clear that law and order must improve significantly. Goals were defined and communicated to the implementing department. The home secretary and DGP formed a team and defined and redefined goals for the field officers. Communication was complete and clearly understood. Lo and behold, within a period of 4-5 years, crime rates went down by 50-60% overall. Governance Entropy decreased from 56% to 29%, and the governance multiplier increased from 1.7 to 3.2. The income per capita increased from 47,000 to 93,000. This specific case validates the hypothesis that good law and order are necessary conditions for income growth. Law and order, as stated above, are comparative to the earlier years. For example, people avoided night travel in the nighttime, which improved during Yogi's regime. There is evidence that people feel safe travelling during the night. Law and order is about safe travel and safe neighborhoods. Without any doubt rule of law gets additional strength from the providers of freedom and justice in addition to safe travel. One fact that people, however, are not happy is about registering treason criminal cases against peaceful protestors. One may say, law and order improved, but the rule of law issues still remain in the UP state. The point is, a little change in the law and order situation has reflected upon the per capita income, which is consistent with the hypothesis that improvement in the rule of law increases income. The state of the rule of law in UP again (October 5, 2021) has taken a hit at deteriorating law and order situation at Lakhimpur farmers' protesting and politically connected persons mowing their vehicle into the protesters killing farmers.

Leave a Copy Behind

For continuity, training and mentoring subordinates to be leader-ready are crucial. Commitment to training and education is a good strategy for the democratic institution to survive and thrive. The mentor and the mentee share knowledge that takes the leadership next high. It would be disastrous for a country if a situation arises 'after they who'? For the self-growth of employees, a delegation of power plays a role in making them responsible and accountable. It builds trust and confidence. I had an opportunity to serve in a university in India. It was more than crystal clear that the predecessor had combined all the powers, especially financials, in him. "It's overwhelming for approving the purchases of a pair of pens and for purchasing ink refills for the printers," I thought.

During a meeting of the professors, a question was raised (grievance), "it was operationally challenging to continue without printers rendered unfunctional because of ink refills." "Raising an indent and getting the refill is an arduous project," one professor said. I nodded in agreement. "But why can't you purchase it in time?" I asked. Everybody else joined him in chorus, "we don't have the financial power to purchase one.". It was informed that the department head had only rupees 500 (~10 us dollars) power to purchase supplies. "It's ridiculous," I said. "How much do you need that would avoid any problems in the future?" I asked. They said five thousand is good enough. I asked what about ten thousand to take care of inflation in future years. They all agreed, and delegation of financial power was complete and done with their partnership in the decision-making. It built trust and confidence in doing business and leading. It saved wasteful costs and time. Delegation of power helps a leader as well as the employees.

Delegation of power is one element in preparing employees for taking responsibility. The crucial part, however, is training and education. An authentic leader would look beyond their term. A leader would nurture the second-in-command to be first-in-command ready. The story of life helps in understanding it better. The property of life is that couples leave copies behind for humanity to survive and thrive for continuity. It's a life cycle. Reproduction is an integral part of the biological cycle. Kids are nurtured to take the command of the family to continue.

Similarly, in any organization, to continue and survive, a second-in-command must be nurtured to be first-in-command ready to take on the responsibilities of the leadership. Leaving a copy behind is a good strategy. This strategy is consistent with natural laws. In a scenario of the absence of a copy and the leaders getting rendered non-functional because of one reason or other, there would be a void. Void generates uncertainty, and uncertainty generates entropy. Entropy means disorder and lost paradise. The winning strategy is to keep the second-in-command ready to take over as the first-in-command and lead seamlessly. Winning strategies are the craftwork of leading effectively. Being aware of what works and what works authentically helps. A leader works with people as people and never uses them as objects for personal gains; they focus on shared goals and communicate truthfully and transparently. An authentic leader is always there for the people. Good governance and the authenticity of leadership are consistent. If the leaders shed their real self and work for personal gains, governance takes a hit.

Good Governance

Human beings aspire to live decent life with freedom. According to Locke, "Where there is no law, there is no freedom (free from violence, fear, intimidation, and other demeaning acts)." The presence of good governance with authentic leadership can enforce the rule of law and bring prosperity to the people. Elite has all the motivation to remain saddled in power positions. However, alert citizens can keep them within bounds by becoming guard rails of liberty and democracy. Peoples' participation in democracies is critical to keep authoritarian tendencies of inauthentic leaders away. Complete presence of governance and complete absence of governance can be equally problematic and ill libertarian. For example, historically, in earlier societies of hunter-gatherers and pastoral existence, life was solitary, nasty, poor, brutish, and short (in Hobbs words). Hobbs reasoned that a central authority is necessary to regulate the brutish behavior of the people arising from human nature. A central authority, too, becomes nasty and brutish if not checked. That's why we have a system of checks and balances. It's another story, though, that checks and balances merge into one leviathan to inflict misery to its people, and liberty is taken away for personal gains.

The fact of the matter is that a necessary condition for a life to exist is food, shelter, and security. Even today, in the so-called civilized world, humans do live a life of scarcity and insecurity. The complete presence of government can be problematic if it becomes out of control. For example, Syria, Libya, Nigeria, and many other authoritarian countries keep people under complete dominance; liberty is nowhere to be seen. The complete presence of government, if it enforces laws, provides for basic infrastructure, education, and health, helps a decent life to its people, and guarantees freedom as against the dominance in the authoritarian regimes. If history is any guide, alert citizens would rise to the occasion and take back their life from such rogue regimes. Authentic leadership can win the trust and cooperation of the people and is a winning strategy for good governance. In the following figure 13.2 a relationship has been put in the form of a 2*2 matrix. On the vertical side, it is governance variable. Governance ranges from high to low, high being on the vertical top. Similarly, the second variable of informed people (how well informed the people are) is placed on the horizontal axis, ranging from low to high on the right side.

FIGURE 13.2

Governance High

high on governance, low on informed people **3** **Authoritarianism**	high on governance, high on informed people **4** **Good Governance**
low on governance, low on informed people **1** **Tribalism**	low on governance, high on informed people **2** **Stateless Society**

Information High

As depicted in Figure 13.2, good governance results from the complete presence of government for the enforcement of the rule of law and providing for infrastructure, education, and health. Ungoverned spaces, as has been explained in chapter 2, aren't efficient. Additionally, at the same time, alert citizens' presence is critical. Uninformed citizens, not participating in democratic processes, have the potential of being dominated by the elite class and put liberty and prosperity at risk. Under such circumstances outcome is equally worse as in the case of absence of governance. If people are not well informed and a simultaneous complete absence of governance exists, the outcome would be disastrous, and it would have all the semblance of tribalism where groups and subgroups keep fighting for dominance and results in violence and hunger. For example, the outcome in the Congo's tribalism is violence and conflict; people have bare existence; hunger is perennial, and life expectancy is dismal. In Nigeria, too, facts are similar. Afghanistan is facing the same circumstances.

If the government is too powerful and citizens aren't well informed and fail to provide pushbacks, it morphs into an authoritarian regime – despotic—for example, North Korea. Syria has done no good to its citizens. A good governance regime is possible only with a high presence of governance for enforcing the rule of law and the complete presence of alert citizens to keep the authoritarian dispositions of the elected people in check. It's ironic, though. People who get to the top positions through democratic processes start using them for personal gains. Checks and balances institutional mechanisms seem to combine (police, politicians, civil servants become complicit) for elite's dominance. Only alert and informed people can stop this. Historically, a small number of the organized and well-informed elite have dominated the unorganized and not-so-informed majority. Why is it so? Simple: if interpreted in natural sciences terms, a small number of micro-states have less entropy than large numbers; information reduces entropy.

On the other hand, a large number of unorganized and less informed people would certainly have higher entropy. Outcome: the dominance of a small, well-informed group. Alert and well-informed citizens can only reduce entropy.

Call it pushback; call it checks and balances. It's only people who can make it possible to keep liberty alive. Solon, the Greek Statesman, created democratic institutions for enforcing the rule of law. Simultaneously, he created mechanisms to have control over these institutions with the objective of controlling the elite and the state. He abolished pawning and even legislated Hubris law to minimize the dominance of the elite. Aristotle agreed with the notion of empowering the common person. The question is, what does it take to empower? Only legislation doesn't do the job. What makes it possible is people's continuous participation and active checks and pushbacks on transgressions of the elite for personal gains. Rule of Law brings about prosperity, and prosperity keeps people active participants to make it a virtuous cycle. Good governance and peoples' active participation are a winning strategy.

If I Were Taliban, What Would be My Winning Strategy?

Taliban means students in Afghanistan. Taliban also means seeking knowledge. Violence seems inconsistent with the very idea of word 'Taliban.' To solve issues at hand, I would seize the day by using natural science laws' insights. One such insight is entropy: many microstates increase entropy, and one macrostate brings order back. In Afghanistan, we have an entropy problem – it's remarkably high. (https://leadershipgov.com/Entropy)

The question is how to solve Afghanistan Problem in terms of the Natural science law of entropy? As of today (August 2021), foreign forces are leaving the country without any administrative functionality. Status: many microstate social systems in one country. Lots of polarization, lots of uncertainty. How to reduce entropy, then? The answer lies in stabilizing the micro-social systems in the country. **Entropy reducing agents in social systems are** knitting together micro-social systems, information, communication, reduction in violence, reduction in uncertainty, cutting on ignorance, reduction in polarization, reduction in divisive forces, and the rule of law toward one governance system.

Hey Taliban, congratulations on your victory and getting back your country from foreign forces. But it's a big BUT, follow natural science laws and make your country great. Yes, reduce entropy in your country community. **You made a good start**: announced amnesty for all; announced education for the women. Now move to the next steps: say it, again and again, education is the information builder in society, and you are for it. You would teach your girls and keep them in the workforce. In the modern world, women are breadwinners, and they do it more effectively than men. One literate woman in the house has a multiplier effect in bringing education to family and community. Reduce entropy by knitting together all the Shuras in your country and make one Super Shura (Shura means community) lead the country out of the chaos. Outsource, if you need to, administrative skills.

Entropy can be reduced by sewing together microsocial systems into one macro-social system. This is possible only through micro-social systems' cooperation, communication, message clarity, and uncertainty reduction. Violence increases entropy. Reduce it by talking and sitting together. You have this incredible skill built in your Shura Culture. This is your strength. Use it. Build one Super Shura who trusts in education (information reduces entropy), human rights, civil rights, non-violence (violence increases entropy; your goal demands reduction). Why use guns against your own people? Use them for military purposes.

As explained in Figure 13.2, the Afghanistan case clearly falls in the first quadrant: less government and less informed people. In such a situation, many micro-social systems exist, which is the case now (August 2021) in Afghanistan. The strategy lies in bringing more governance and making people more informed. How do you do it? It can be accomplished by the application of natural science laws to social systems and by reducing entropy. Informed people in the government would reduce entropy.

Transparency is the key that helps entropy reduction. To have a stateless society, the necessary condition, as in quadrant 2, is highly informed people. And that is a rarity. Then the best option available to a society to manage itself efficiently and for the prosperity of all is to have a quadrant 4 condition: highly educated people with government's regulation like an umpire in a soccer game. Sports don't happen without an umpire and people watching in attendance: rules of the game clearly defined, understood, and communicated to all the participants. Presence of impartial umpire, and people's watch make a winning strategy. So is the case for any governance system to be of any worth, it must be transparent, it must have the rule of law, well defined and well understood by the people and the state actors, and it must have a system of checks and balances. Higher the entropy in a social system, lower is the multiplier effect of its intended decisions. It's far easier said than done. But the solution lies only in learning from history and successful patterns of good governance. For the prosperity of people, the rule of law is a necessary condition, and a government is good only if it provides for liberty, justice and freedom for all and work on the issues of public service. Authentic leadership functions under the restraints of accountability.

****

14

Caged Bureaucracy: Learned Helplessness

In the mid-nineties (2020), I attended a training course (Mid-Career) with other IAS officers of vertical construction at IIM Bengaluru. The Professor, who was assigned to deliver discourses on leadership, gave us a test (a psychological personality test) if we were qualified leaders. We all took the test and eagerly waited for the scores who qualified to be a leader, a survivalist, or an innocent lamb. The test outcome was pretty interesting: none qualified to be a leader, the majority turned out to be survivalists (it included me), and a small minority fell (according to the test) into the innocent lambs category. Really, innocent lambs? A few of us, dismissive of the test, argued with the Professor. Professor, in all his humility, stood his ground and explained it was a standardized test. Indeed, the Professor was right. No wonder, with due respect, IAS officers are addressed as Babus. Civil service officers indeed are survivalists and follow cage norms. However, a tiny minority of officers, an almost extinct species of civil service, do stand upright and follow the rule book (constitution) in pursuit of leadership (or innocent lambs?), a role they are supposed to play, appear to break the cage norms. According to NN Vohra, while commenting on the state of officers and the politicians' complicity, such officers are seldom heard again.

According to Reuters (May 9, 2013), the Supreme Court of India described CBI as a "caged parrot' and "its master's voice." Informally, Earlier Directors of CBI admitted that CBI is subject to the influence, Reuter further added to its report. There are checks and balances as per our constitution to keep the democratic institutions alive. However, checks and balances seem to converge and become complicit that hurts authentic leadership. According to Vinod Rai CAG report (09/08/2011), all checks and balances powers seemed to combine and were complicit in the management affairs of Adarsh Co-operative Housing Society, Mumbai. Was the IAS officers' gameplan a survivalist's strategy? It's anybody's guess. None dared seem to have broken the cage norms. Instead, they seem to have jumped on the corruption wagon. Aren't these cage norms consistent with the survivalist personality characterization by the Professor at Bengaluru IIM?

Officers seem to have a preference for safe driving over the righteous course. Many appear to be street smart by choice. Either way, authentic leadership remains elusive.

Earlier societies, and even at some places in modern times, stateless societies do exist and live in small groups usually called clans (civil service in India equivalent: IAS clan), consisting of family and siblings. The economic norms of sharing, right of taking, and obligations of giving prevail. The barter exchange system, too, still is visible in Africa. Even in India, in far rural settings of some states like Bihar and Northeastern states, a barter system exists. Food, shelter, and security are the necessary conditions of life. Where the modern trade system does not reach, local societies are governed by local cage norms. Anybody breaking norms is isolated, ostracized and left alone to fend for their existence. For example, even in the developed state of Haryana, the Khap system still prevails. Norms are handed over down to generations. Despite the existence of democratically elected government, local norms are honored by the village residents: inter-caste and interfaith marriages are resisted, and punishment awarded; Khap (area representative body- a group of few villages) decisions are taken (many a time at odds with the existing government system) for solving local problems and honored locally.

Civil services seem to have cage norms, too: political will prevails over prescribed laws. 'Will to Power' and 'Will to Pleasure' seem to overshadow 'Will to Serve.' What is a cage, though? Cage has boundaries; it has norms. In the IAS clan, broken norms don't go unnoticed: isolated, ostracized, left alone, socially avoided, dumped, seldom heard again. If some officers dare to make the right decisions, with little caring for the status or position of a politician, they are left alone, and fellow officers avoid even talking to them out of fear of revenge by the power at the time. One of the senior officers showing unhappiness over his posting visited Chief Secretary asking for what he liked the best. The officer was advised to visit the CM's kin. The gentleman wasted no time and waited at the door. Later in the years of his retirement, CS expressed his opinion, though, that casteism serves no body. The thing is that they wish to break open the cage; however, they find it safe to navigate (survivalist) and start a cage living subconsciously as a defense mechanism. It's simple. If you trust something is wrong (cognitive dissonance), you change it or justify it. Most often, the latter prevails, and the cage norms are reinforced. Outcome: a handful of the politicians have a free ride.

One of the issues with bureaucracy is the word 'Babu.' Civil servants don't like this word, and politicians and journalists take pleasure in addressing officers as Babu. One of the (dynastic democracy) heir apparent once asked about the characterization of the IAS officers, who are supposed to solve problems and hold integrity as the key element of their service motto. He said, "I will visit a place of my choice. These officers would be standing in queue, supervising water sprinkling to make the venue look good." In other words, he was indicating toward the fact that officers are self-responsible for their plight as they ask for cherry postings. Good officers are called to lead; they don't seek to lead. But, unfortunately, it's a cage norm; "keep the politician happy if need a plum posting." As such, it's not uncommon for the officers to hitch their horses to politicians' wagon. A recent example of registering treason cases against the protestors in India is supportive of the fact that officers seem to follow their political masters blindly.

The tool, the politicians use is "shock and awe." Many local vernacular expressions they use to drive off these trained to "stick-to-law" officers from the right course for their personal gains. One day one of the relatives of a minister asks for a favor from him. He picks up a file and asks his senior-most officer (IAS officer) to get the work done. To temporarily avoid the problem on the other side of the phone, he speaks, "yes, sir, it will be done." Without losing time, the minister calls another minister, and two of them straightaway barge in his office room (IAS officers) with the file and place the file on his table to get it signed. The officer hesitates, and they hound him like coyotes. The thing is officers learn the cage norms of survival by gaining time to handle a situation. But it leads nowhere. The right course is break open the cage, be aware of the processes trickling down the system, define the problem, and talk straight. I am sure people in the seat of power would fall in line consistent with the rule book.

Cage norms are breakable, and the scientific approach helps it. Science laws help to become aware of human existence. Humanity is best served by authentic leadership. If the laws of nature seem to work in the physical systems, why not understand social systems consistent with the natural sciences? Ignorance of nature's phenomenon is an existential threat. Natural laws, which are tried and tested, have applications for social sciences, social ecosystems, and good governance. People somehow have a preference for a street-smart person to move on. But this is a myopic view. Burying head into sand possibly cannot solve lurking problems. Perceiving things as unsolvable and learning to live with them is a dangerous strategy.

Learned Helplessness

The intuitive notion of helplessness is the belief that nothing you do matters. And the response to such a situation results into passivity, why even think about it attitude. They don't have escapable control over the adverse events and outcomes. It's a state of mind in which an organism forced to bear adverse stimuli becomes unwilling to avoid those stimuli. In other words, people or animals start perceiving that bad situations are unchangeable, and they can't escape those. In his book *Helplessness* (1975), Seligman argued that, due to these negative expectations, unwillingness to act surfaces. As a consequence, an individual develops an inability to change their fate. Seligman's theory of helplessness has applications to various fields: human behavior, poverty, academic achievements, and governance.

As for bureaucracy, it's a fact of life that in democracies, there are elected state actors who have their narrow interests (both personal and constituents). According to Aristotle, democracies are fragile, and it happens when democratic institutions are diminished or diluted by the state actors, sitting at the top, for their narrow ends. Once trapped in a complicit situation an officer has no escape route. It's one-drop rule. One misstep; all is finished. For an officer, it's critical to be aware of such entrapments to remain consistent with the rule book. This is what the 'will-to-power' people prey on. They make dossiers, and the righteousness of a serving state actor vanishes. The entire system takes the shape of inescapable existence. The question is how to escape? Or is it a situation of cognitively learned helplessness?

Insights from Neuroscience

Research in neuroscience has evolved, and the idea of learned helplessness has been dug deep down into the physicality of the brain. According to the theory of learned helplessness, it's the profound failure to escape the adverse phenomenon (for officers to be complicit with politicians to survive, transfer industry), and learned helplessness is a cognitive phenomenon.

"Passivity in response to shock is not learned. It is the default, unlearned response to prolonged aversive events, and it is mediated by the serotonergic activity of the dorsal raphe nucleus, which inhibits escape. This passivity can be overcome by learning control, with the activity of the medial prefrontal cortex, which subserves the detection of control, leading to the automatic inhibition of the dorsal raphe nucleus. So, animals learn that they can control aversive events, but the passive failure to learn to escape is an unlearned reaction to prolonged aversive stimulation."

(Psychol Rev. 2016 Jul; 123(4): 349–367. doi: 10.1037/rev0000033)

According to this research, officers certainly have a choice to make up for the losses and can have an escape door. It's simple. The perceived fear of losing is unreal. Politicians don't own the law. They, too, reach the position of power through the democratic mechanisms only. It becomes handy for them if the willing officers serve their personal goals. Over time, it becomes a cage rule: it's the politicians that the officers serve and not the law, which is a toxic construction for both the officers as well as the people they are supposed to serve under the umbrella of the rule of law.

Political leaders often reinforce the cage norms (that they are the boss and not the law) by opening the flood gates of the transfer industry. They demand loyalty to themselves as against loyalty to the rule of law. Recent uttering of the previous CM of the state of Madya Pradesh is cage norm expectations reinforcement only. "The bureaucracy is nothing but meant to pick up our slippers," she said. Really? A similar view of sequaciously serving bureaucrats is often quoted from the state of Tamil Nadu during the regime of late Jayalalitha. It's not uncommon to see officers, even in uniform, touching the feet of political leaders. Are these the cage norms for survival, or do people do it for becoming complicit for personal gains? Either way, leadership is lost. Yes, transferring an officers 'n' number of times puts an inescapable situation. But this situation is controllable, and an escape route is possible. The learned helplessness or passivity to respond to adverse politically triggered events is a dangerous strategy. The naked acts of state actors to extract resources and bribes from the people (a recent example of Mumbai, Home minister and Police commissioner complicit in collecting rents from the small business owners) is consistent with Khaldun's generational theory, which brings nasty trouble to people. According to this theory, the siblings of authoritarian and extractors become insensitive to the state affairs. Their protective self-indulgence leads to corrosive governance. It's not uncommon to notice, in dynastic democracies, siblings of people in power positions have little care for the rule of law. Socio-economic fiber weakens and prosperity disappears. Siblings of the authoritarian regimes surpass their ancestors in delivering cruelties and humiliation to the people they govern. Authentic leadership is the last thing, they know and practice. Personal predilections are the forces that drive them at the cost of misery to common people. According to the religious book 'Bhagavat Gita,' why should even a person hoard wealth when their bad siblings are going to burn it? If the siblings are good, they will have enough energy and prudence to make it. In other words, bad governance for bad objectives is bad for everyone.

Allegory of Good Government

For good governance, consul (to the leaders in power position) of independent, competent, and integrity driven officers is a necessary condition. In a caged bureaucracy, civil servants are used as tools of oppression. Machiavellian rule of fear serves no one. In democratic construction, the allegory of good governance, depicted in the frescoes of Sienese state in Italy of 1338 is relevant. For liberty, peace, and prosperity of the people, it's the will of the people that matters. In the following Figure 14.1, the fresco painting (painted 1338-1339, by Ambrogio Lorenzetti, Italian Painter) offers insights for good governance. The fresco painting is in Piazza del Campo, Siena. Palazzo Publlico housed Siena's government. In the painting it would be noticed that the ruler is surrounded by three consuls on the right and three consuls on the left. The public is in the foreground and the ruling class is in the background. It seems to signify the fact that the people of Siena had the final say in the matters of governance. They participated and appointed good consuls to keep restraint on the rulers of the day.

Peace and justice was important to them. For them it provided prosperity.

Figure 14.1 (source: google.com)

Artistic representation in the painting stands for Fortitude, Prudence, and Peace on the left and Temperance, Justice, and Generosity on the right. In this fresco, rulers in the background points to the fact that peoples' 'Will' prevail. "Will-to-Power" (rulers) is in the background. It signifies liberty and the rule of law. As explained in Chapter 2, the rule of law has a positive correlation with prosperity. In Siena government dispensation, too, communes were prosperous. It only reinforces the point that caged bureaucracy serves no one. It's the good governance by informed peoples' participation that matters. If bureaucracy is used as a tool to suppress the legitimate concerns of the people, the government no longer remains authentic. Good governance is dispensed by the will of the consuls (justice, liberty, freedom, democratic institutions) instead of the rulers. The government functions with restraint. According to the traveler Benjamin of Tudela during his journey through Pisa (1165), "They possess neither king nor prince to govern them, but only the judges appointed by themselves." This only signifies the fact that wherever the 'rule of law' and 'will-of-the-people' prevail, prosperity is the outcome. The role of the bureaucracy (civil service officers) lie in authentic consul to the elected state actors in the modern day republics. The only cage norms (if any) for them are provisions, as enshrined in the constitution. Certainly, officers aren't caged; they are there to assist (consul) the leadership elected by the will of the people. For good governance "Allegory of Good Government" offers light in the cloudy days for the democracies on the cliff.

****

ACKNOWLEDGMENTS

It takes an effort to author a book. In this effort, the author is not the only one. Many others are essential contributors. I am indebted to my family members, who patiently took all my idiosyncratic ways of asking them their views on what I was writing. They all have been an inspiration and a joy in my life. This book is about leadership from family matters to governance at the state/country level: whatever the story, leadership matters, and people surrounding the leader matter. I am grateful to all those who supported and corrected me at the various stages of the project: the very idea of writing, editing, assisted editing, and preprinting. Vikrant Malik looked patient in his impatience for helping individual chapters in one combined document. Dr, Shireen explained entropy in terms of the second law of thermodynamics, human anatomy, neuroscience and helped me develop alternative cover pages. Special thanks to Gurpreet and his team for designing/developing the website (leadershipgov.com) for computer applications that the book explains.

I express my gratitude to friends, colleagues, and seniors who took time off to look at the manuscript chapters and offering excellent suggestions. Furthermore, my thanks go to many people associated with this project to collect data from secondary sources and tabulate it. Their efforts included taking printouts and again inserting the amended changes. Finally, I especially thank the participants for answering the quiz questions as per their best intelligent guesses from their years of unique experience in their respective professions and lives.

Singh. Maha

INDEX

A
Accumulation, 68
Acemoglu, 16
Acquired information, 72
Adarsh society example, 207
Adolf Hitler, 9, 116
Afghanistan, 225, 228, 230
Afghanistan Problem, 228
Agra, 106
Ahmedabad IIM, 122
AJ Oswald, 99
Albert, 73
algos, rogue, 137
algos pool, 138
allegory of good governance, 244
Amazon, 58
analysis
  cost-benefit, 41
  impact diamond, 165, 172–73
analysis toolbox, 171
Anasazi, 26
Apollinaire, Guillaume, 101

application of natural science laws to social systems, 230
Arab Springs, 50
Aristotle, 5, 227, 240
Assam, 160
assessing governance, 182, 186
Assessing Leaders, 189
authenticity, 222
authentic leadership, 1, 3, 8, 12, 43, 46, 126, 128, 191, 193, 222–23, 234–35, 238
Authentic leadership functions, 232
Authentic leadership's essence, 11
Authentic leaders obsessively, 32
authoritarian, 168, 243
authoritarian countries, 223
authoritarian dispositions, 226
authoritarian measures, 121
Autocrats, 17
automatic inhibition, 241

autopilot, 69, 135–36, 141–42, 144
Aware, 61

B
Babas, 65, 81
Bangladesh, 58
behavior, 5, 40–42, 76, 85, 119, 134
Berlin, 106
Bhagavat Gita, 243
Bhai sahibs, 81
Bible, 23, 116
Bihar, 20, 160, 235
biological molecules-DNA, 72
biology, 72
  molecular, 131
black swan events, 148, 150–52, 155–57, 160, 162
Black Swan Events and Leadership, 148
Bombay, 55
brain, 64, 66, 68–70, 82, 90–93, 95, 131–45, 155, 240
brain anatomy, 66, 70
brain function, 90, 94
brain mapping, 64, 70
brain plasticity, 70
bureaucracy, 119, 207, 237, 240, 242, 246
Bush, George, 81
businessperson, 176, 178

C
cage norm expectations reinforcement, 242
cage norms, 233–34, 236–38, 242, 246
Canada, 55, 59, 104
capitalism, 27, 47
CBI, 61, 234
Charlotte Prozan, 85
Churchill, 9

Winston, 35
Civil service culture, 208
civil services, 31, 164, 200, 206–7, 234–36
Clinton, Bill, 180–81
codes
  developmental stage, 143
  genetic, 141
  hard, 141
  new, 143
  right, 144
  subroutine, 91
cognitive bias, 71, 155
cognitive heuristics, 87
cognitive science unleashes, 133
Collective ownership, 43
constitution, 15, 62, 132, 199, 206, 234, 246
consuls, 244, 246
Contingency theory, 7
Costa Ricans, 112
covid, 47, 111, 150, 196
  current pandemic, 81
COVID-19, 120, 153
COVID-19 pandemic, 151
coyotes, wall street, 108
crime rate, increasing, 165
Crime Rate and House-Hold Income, 21
Crises, 149
crisis, humanitarian, 123
Crisis and black swan events, 157
crisis handling, 3
cronyism, 31, 167–68, 173, 181, 187, 200
Cross-Road-Moments, 128
Cruz, Ted, 150
culture, work-horse, 113

D
de facto pull strings, 123

defined goals, 12, 164
  well-defined, 216
Defining Moments Shape
    Leaders, 10
De Jure, 121
Delhi city, 109
democratic institutions, strong,
    66–67, 96
deplorability forces, 102
deplorables, 99, 101–2, 104,
    106–7
Deploville, 22, 101
DGP Julio Ribeiro, 166
Dharavi shanty area, 55
DHL, 58
dignity, 48, 53, 76
Disinfectant machines, 203
Disraeli, Benjamin, 37
dissonance, 94
  cognitive, 71, 129, 236
domino, 185
  falling, 185
  next, 185
domino effect, 76, 182, 185
dorsal raphe nucleus, 241
double-strand breaks (DSB),
    132
DSB (double-strand breaks),
    132
DSM, 83–84
dysfunctional behaviors, 117

E
ego, 42, 116, 122
Elements of Awareness, 66
elements of well-defined goals
    and clear
    communication, 217
Elitism, 48
Elsbeth Johnson, 9
Elvin, 73

empathy, 3–4, 8, 42, 44, 81,
    83–84, 94–95, 132–33,
    191
empathy levels, 94
Enlightenment, 14
entropy, 61, 72, 111, 126, 133,
    170–71, 178, 182–98,
    204, 221, 226–31
  estimate leadership, 189
  reducing, 230
  zero, 183–84, 188
entropy event, 186
entropy in communication,
    204
entropy problem, 228
Entropy reducing agents in
    social systems, 228
entropy reduction, 173, 231
environmental clues, 91
environmental problems, 26
environmental substrate, 93
  unique, 91
epidemiologist/scientists, 126
escape route, 240, 242
Ethiopia famine, 26
Eurich, Tasha, 63
Europe, 56, 104
  medieval, 148
Evolutionary Dispositions, 17
existence, human, 152, 238

F
FDR, 7
FEMA, 156
Fibonacci, 50
Field Marshal Manek Shaw,
    10
Figures for India, 53
financial anxieties, 45, 193
financial inequalities, 195
Financial Model, 213
first-in-command, 220–21
fiscal policy, 197

Fiscal response goals, 197
Franco, Francisco, 9, 116
Francois, 9, 115
Franklin, Benjamin, 160
Freedom of speech, 163
free will, 67, 69, 89–93, 95
Freewill, 142
French poet, 101
French revolution, 50
Freud's theory, 5

G
Gandhi Ji, 1, 12, 29, 75, 101, 109
GDP, 2, 97, 109, 112, 195, 198
godmen, 65
Goldman Sachs, 113–14
Goleman, 4
good governance, 2, 14–15, 103, 166, 169, 172, 174, 181, 183–84, 222, 224, 227, 244, 246
Good Government, 244
Good officers, 237
governance ecosystem, 164, 184
governance entropy, 172, 174, 178, 183, 186, 189, 214, 217
Governance Impact Diamond, 172–73
governance instruments, 163
governance multiplier, 169, 171, 173–74, 186, 217
government, allegory of good, 244, 246
Great leaders, 205

H
happiness, 2, 62, 97, 99–103, 106–7, 109–10, 112, 216
happiness and beauty, 101
happiness and dollar income, 102
happiness and success, 103
Hare Psychopathy Checklist, 94
Hare's scale, 193
Harvard, 49, 84
Harvard Business School, 45
Harvard University, 146
Haryana, 94, 161, 169, 212–14, 235
Haryana's state, 23
hazardous debris, 35
helplessness, 239, 241
High on well-defined goals, 216
Hitler, 83, 94, 193
Hobbs, 222
Hobbs words, 222
Hobson's choice, 129
Hockaday, 5
holy grail, 44, 100
Home Secretary, 30, 214, 217
homo sapiens, 1, 41, 62
Hook, Sandy, 156
hubris, 8, 49, 61–62, 75, 78–83, 85–90, 92, 94, 96, 139, 162
    corporate-level, 87
Hubris and Free Will, 89
hubris a personality disorder, 81
hubris disorder, 85
hubris-laden heads, 135
hubris manifests, 78
hubris personality disorder, 82
hubristic, 86
Hubristic decision, 83
humanism, 132
Human societies, 26
human trafficking color, 104

I

ignorance, 40, 43, 61–62, 71–72, 75, 77, 184, 190, 192, 202–3, 229
Indian, 62
Indian billionaires, 53
inequality, 27–28, 30, 50, 53–57, 59–60, 81, 109, 154, 195–97
inequality and growth, 196
Inequality and Underpaid workers, 52
information molecules, 73
innate instinctive tendencies, 41
inner diamond, improved, 173
insights for good governance, 244
instinct, 39, 41–42, 44, 72, 191
Instinct and intelligence, 72
instinct and intelligence scale, 42
intelligence, 41–42, 44, 72, 191
intimidation style, 46
Iraq, 117
irrationality, 155
Islamophobic, 107
Italian Painter, 244
Italy, 9, 98, 116, 244

J
Jakarta, 106
James, William, 139
jeopardy zone, 74
Jhopar-Patties, 106
judiciary, 165, 167–68, 171, 187–88

K
Keynesian multipliers, 179, 186
keystones, 12, 164, 167, 189
Khap system, 235

killer whales, 143
Kill Hubris, 92
Krugman, Paul, 58, 112

L
labs, fMRI, 142
law
  legislated Hubris, 227
  natural sciences, 188
  nature's, 54–55, 68, 182–83
  rule of, 13–15, 20–22, 30–31, 33–34, 103, 108–10, 163–68, 175, 179, 181, 187, 199–200, 217–18, 225–27, 231, 242–43, 245–46
law and order, 1, 14–16, 18–20, 32–33, 51, 178, 207, 214, 217–18
law-and-order, 15
Law and Order and Income, 18
law-and-order deficit states, 18
law-and-order issue, 15
Lawful Governance Spawns Growth, 13
law of thermodynamics and entropy, 72
law&order, 22
law&order Line Fit Plot, 22
Law&Order score and Nominal Income, 19
law parameters, 217
laws of nature, 238
leaders
  hubris-ridden, 79
  narcissist, 120–21
leadership, 1–14, 20, 31–32, 34–35, 40, 47–48, 61–63, 80–83, 103, 113–14, 126–29, 131, 144–45, 148–52, 157–59, 162–64, 199–200, 211, 213–16, 221–22

crisis management, 152
good, 14, 19, 88, 126–27
hubristic, 82–84
narcissism-toxic, 118
narcissistic, 17
strategic, 152–53
sublime, 12
transactional, 152
Leadership & Winning Strategies, 199
leadership assessment, 180
leadership characteristics, 79
leadershipgov.com, 169, 188, 192, 194
Leadership Productivity Multiplier Factors, 190
leadership's success, 100
leadership style matters, 7
leadership styles, 6, 10, 80, 127, 134, 153
Learned behavior, 41
rogue, 141
level of leaders, 1
level of leadership, 1
Libya, 223
life equation, 32, 67–68, 73
life evaluations, 109–10
life expectancy, 225
life function, max, 67
life function's value, 75
life function value, 75
life Max function, 110
life of happiness, 109
lockdowns, 120, 123, 127, 194, 202
Lockdowns of economies, 195
Locke, 222
Lorenz curve, steep, 57

M

machine, fMRI, 64, 88, 90, 133, 135, 142
Madya Pradesh, 242

Mahul, 27
Main Street, 82, 121
Mao, 83, 115
Mao Zedong, 9
Marginal sensitivity to safety, 165
Mark Twain, 71
Martin Luther King, 49
Marx, 5
Karl, 100
Massachusetts Boston, 145
matrix, i, 41
Maya, 26
measure, electricity delivery system power factor, 170
measure governance entropy, 186
measurement of entropy, 183
Measurement of Happiness, 109
Measurement of leadership for good governance, 2
Measuring decisions, 164
Meritocracy, 49
Mexicans' happiness, 112
Mexico, 150
micro-social systems, 228, 230
microstates, 228
mindfulness, leader's, 129
Miserability level, 174
mortality rate, 120
MP, 196, 211
MSS, 165–66, 171
multiplier, 166, 169, 173–74, 186
good, 171
multiplier effect, 169, 178, 185, 196, 229, 231
Mumbai episode, 30
Mussolini, Benito, 9, 116
Mussoorie, 28

N
narcissism, 85, 116
Narratives of charismatic leaders, 4
Nassim Nicholas Taleb, 148
National Human, 124
natural laws, 31, 132–33, 171, 182, 186, 221, 238
Natural science law, 228–30
Natural science law of entropy, 228
Neanderthals, 62
neoteny, 11, 44
nepotism, 17–18, 31, 167–68, 173, 181, 187, 200
nepotism and cronyism, 168, 173, 187
neural pathways, 131, 139–40, 144–45
neurodegeneration, 132
neurodiversity, 137
neurogeneration, 140
Neurological insights, 137
Neurological insights help, 136
neurological pathways, 134, 136
neuron pathways, 70
neurons, 66, 69–70, 92, 133–34, 139, 142
neuroscience, 88, 131–33, 142, 145, 147, 240
Neuroscience and Leadership, 131
neuroscience experiment, 95
neuroscience knowledge, 144
neuroscientists, 64, 69–70, 88–90, 92, 133–35, 138
New Zealand, 127, 159, 203
Nicolae Ceausescu, 9, 115
NN Vohra, 30–31, 61, 234
Noble laureate Einstein, 134
non-violence, 230

normal distribution, 149
norms, local, 235
North America, 56
Northeast, 23
North Korea, 9, 15, 115, 226

O
OECD countries, 22

P
painting, fresco, 244
Panchkula, 161
pandemic management, 159
Pandemic New Zealand, 191
passivity, 239, 241–42
pathology, 76
patterns of good governance, 231
people-centric, 6–7
People want their life back, 194
PE ratio, 54
  historical good, 54
Perfect market competition, 184
performance standards, 180
Peril, 130
personality disorder, 83–86
physical systems, 184, 190, 238
physicists, 72
physics law of entropy, 171
planning, 4, 13, 140, 160–62
plasticity, 140
Plato, 5
polarization, 228–29
power factor, 170, 183–84
productivity, 176
prudence, 168, 243, 245
psychiatrists, 52, 64, 133
psychiatry, 64, 120
psychoanalysis, 5
psychoanalysts, 133

psychological illness, 91
psychological issues, 120
psychologists, 52, 88, 102
   clinical, 84
psychology, 63, 139
   clinical, 131
psychopathic undertones, 52
psychopath's delight, 52
psychopathy, 95, 193, 210
psychopathy scale, 193
psychotherapist, 85
psychoville, 129
Publilius Syrus, 157
Punjab University, 211

Q
Queens, 3

R
Ralph Waldo Emerson, 186
randomness, 111, 182
ratio, golden, 50, 55
RBI, 202
redundancy, 156–57
REED, 17
regeneration, 139
regenesis, 73–74
regions, amygdala, 64
Reuters, 234
rewriting codes, 143
Ribeiro, Julio, 30–31, 34
righteousness, 65, 240
rights, human, 116, 230
Rio-de-Janeiro, 106
risk, 26, 103, 106, 151, 155, 157, 181, 225
risk avoidance, 156
risk management, 148
Romania, 9, 115
Routines and subroutines
   impact, 95
rubric, 61, 73

Rule of Law and House-Hold
   Income, 20
Rule of Law and House-Hold
   Income in OECD
   countries, 22
runoff, 161–62
Russia, 9, 56, 116

S
safety, 14, 20, 23, 25, 30, 32, 62, 67–68, 73–74, 163–66, 174–75
safety of life, 30
Sahib, 39
science genesis, 75
score, weighted average, 187
Self-awareness of humans, 68
Self-awareness of nature's life
   phenomenon, 68
Seligman's theory, 239
Shakespearean, 75
Shakespearian sound, 73
Shared information, 61
Shiller, Robert J., 99
Shouganai, 144
Shura Culture, 230
Shuras, 229
Siena, 244
Siena government
   dispensation, 245
Sienese state, 244
Singapore, 104, 196–97, 203
socialism, 59
social mobility, 56, 59
Socio-economic fiber, 243
Socratic, 62, 70
Socratic inquiry, 77
Socratic inquiry method, 63
Socratic world of truth, 65
Soviet Union, 150
stimuli, 41, 69, 91, 141, 239
story of life, 73, 220

strategy, 31, 37, 155–57, 200–201, 203–5, 208, 210, 221, 230
  applied, 3
  dangerous, 209, 239, 243
  defining, 215
  deliberate, 89
  employee-focused, 210
  excellent, 208
  good, 210, 219, 221
  good leadership, 198, 208
  right, 213
  simple, 82
  survivalist's, 234
strategy works, 214
structures, administrative ecosystem's, 189
Super Shura, 229–30
survival level income, bare, 30
sustainable development, 26
swan, 151
  black, 148, 157, 160
Swart, 140
SWAT team, 201
Sweden, 197
Syria, 223, 226
system, central nervous, 131

T
Taiwan, 204
Takeaway, 103
Taliban, 228–29
Talk Straight, 201
Tamil Nadu, 242
task-centric, 7
TD Garden Boston, 145
theory, trait, 6
tools, 70, 74, 76, 141, 144–45, 165–66, 171, 181–82, 237, 244, 246
Toxic, 42
toxicity, 28, 43, 115, 118, 120, 125, 192–93

Toxicity of leadership, 114
toxic leadership, 113, 115, 117, 121, 124–25, 128, 155
Toxic leaders intimidate subordinates and extract, 126
toxins, 82, 210
Toyota leadership model, 43
Toyota model, 205
Toyota's Model, 205
Tragedy of Hubris, 86
tragedy of ungoverned spaces, 25
traits, 6–7, 11, 67, 76, 84, 116, 190
tribalism, 18, 30, 125, 224–25
truth of happiness, 62, 100
truth of leadership, 62
truth of life, 62

U
Underpaid workers, 52
unexpected events, 153–54, 162, 201
  extreme, 149
UNFCCC, 152
ungoverned spaces, 23, 25, 225
Uninformed citizens, 225
useful work, 170, 172, 183–84, 190
Uttarakhand, 152

V
Vinod Rai, 31, 207
Vinod Rai CAG report, 234

W
wages, poverty-level, 52
Wall-Mart, 58
Wall Street Journal, 127
Washington, 115

water, runoff, 161
wealth, concentration of, 52, 56
wealth gap, 52
Weber, Max, 5
White House, 114, 120
will-of-the-people, 246
will to Pleasure, 236
will to Serve, 236
winners, botched noble prize, 143

Y
Yogi, 32, 34, 217
Yogi's regime, 218

www.ingramcontent.com/pod-product-compliance
Lightning Source LLC
Chambersburg PA
CBHW031612210526
45464CB00004B/1539